The Smallest Hope

THE AZRIELI SERIES OF HOLOCAUST SURVIVOR MEMOIRS: PUBLISHED TITLES

ENGLISH TITLES

The Smallest Hope

Jack Klajman

THE AZRIELI FOUNDATION · www.azrielifoundation.org

A version of Jack Klajman's memoir was previously published as *Out of the Ghetto* by the publisher Vallentine Mitchell. Permission for this new edition was granted by Vallentine Mitchell and Ed Klajman.

Cover design and book design by Mark Goldstein · Cover photo colourized by Mark Goldstein. Original black-and-white photo can be found on page 176 · Interior map by Julie Witmer Custom Map Design · Endpaper maps by Martin Gilbert.

Photos on pages 172 and 176 courtesy of the United States Holocaust Memorial Museum. Photo on page 184 originally published in the *London Free Press*. Material republished with the express permission of: London Free Press, a division of Postmedia Network Inc.

LIBRARY AND ARCHIVES CANADA CATALOGUING IN PUBLICATION

The smallest hope / Jack Klajman.
    Klajman, Jack, 1931–2019 author. Azrieli Foundation, publisher.
The Azrieli series of Holocaust survivor memoirs; XV
Includes bibliographical references and index.
Canadiana (print) 20230219721 · Canadiana (ebook) 20230219748
ISBN 9781998880058 (softcover) · ISBN 9781998880072 (PDF)
ISBN 9781998880065 (EPUB)

LCSH: Klajman, Jack, 1931–2019 LCSH: Jews — Poland — Warsaw — Biography. LCSH: Holocaust, Jewish (1939-1945) — Poland — Warsaw — Personal narratives. LCSH: Jewish children in the Holocaust — Poland — Warsaw — Biography. LCSH: Warsaw (Poland) — History — Warsaw Ghetto Uprising, 1943. LCSH: Warsaw (Poland) — Biography.

LCC DS135.P63 K564 2023   DDC 940.53/18092—dc23

MIX
Paper | Supporting
responsible forestry
FSC
www.fsc.org   FSC® C004191

PRINTED IN CANADA

The Azrieli Foundation's Holocaust Survivor Memoirs Program

Naomi Azrieli, Publisher

Jody Spiegel, Program Director
Arielle Berger, Managing Editor
Catherine Person, Manager and Editor of French Translations
Catherine Aubé, Editor of French Translations
Matt Carrington, Editor
Devora Levin, Editor and Special Projects Coordinator
Marc-Olivier Cloutier, Manager of Education Initiatives
Nadine Auclair, Educator
Michelle Sadowski, Educator
Elin Beaumont, Community and Education Initiatives
Elizabeth Banks, Curator and Archivist

Mark Goldstein, Art Director

Contents

Series Preface:
In their own words. . .

In telling these stories, the writers have liberated themselves. For so many years we did not speak about it, even when we became free people living in a free society. Now, when at last we are writing about what happened to us in this dark period of history, knowing that our stories will be read and live on, it is possible for us to feel truly free. These unique historical documents put a face on what was lost, and allow readers to grasp the enormity of what happened to six million Jews — one story at a time.

David J. Azrieli, C.M., C.Q., M.Arch
Holocaust survivor and founder, The Azrieli Foundation

Since the end of World War II, approximately 40,000 Jewish Holocaust survivors have immigrated to Canada. Who they are, where they came from, what they experienced and how they built new lives for themselves and their families are important parts of our Canadian heritage. The Azrieli Foundation's Holocaust Survivor Memoirs Program was established in 2005 to preserve and share the memoirs written by those who survived the twentieth-century Nazi genocide of the Jews of Europe and later made their way to Canada. The memoirs encourage readers to engage thoughtfully and critically with the complexities of the Holocaust and to create meaningful connections with the lives of survivors.

Millions of individual stories are lost to us forever. By preserving the stories written by survivors and making them widely available to a broad audience, the Azrieli Foundation's Holocaust Survivor Memoirs Program seeks to sustain the memory of all those who perished at the hands of hatred, abetted by indifference and apathy. The personal accounts of those who survived against all odds are as different as the people who wrote them, but all demonstrate the courage, strength, wit and luck that it took to prevail and survive in such terrible adversity. The memoirs are also moving tributes to people — strangers and friends — who risked their lives to help others, and who, through acts of kindness and decency in the darkest of moments, frequently helped the persecuted maintain faith in humanity and courage to endure. These accounts offer inspiration to all, as does the survivors' desire to share their experiences so that new generations can learn from them.

The Holocaust Survivor Memoirs Program collects, archives and publishes select survivor memoirs and makes the print editions available free of charge to educational institutions and Holocaust-education programs across Canada. They are also available for sale online to the general public. All revenues to the Azrieli Foundation from the sales of the Azrieli Series of Holocaust Survivor Memoirs go toward the publishing and educational work of the memoirs program.

The Azrieli Foundation would like to express appreciation to the following people for their invaluable efforts in producing this book: Chochana Boukhobza, Jocelyn Bourque, Stewart Cass of Vallentine Mitchell, Virginia Clark, Stephanie Corazza, Mark Duffus (Maracle Inc.), Judith Earnshaw, Barbara Engelking, Jess Klaassen-Wright, Joëlle Perelberg-Houriez, Rosie Whitehouse and the team at Second Story Press.

Editorial Note

This updated edition of Jack Klajman's memoir contains a new introduction, afterword, map, glossary and photo section. The memoir contains terms, concepts and historical references that may be unfamiliar to the reader. English translations of foreign-language words and terms have been added to the text or as footnotes. The editors of this memoir have worked to maintain the author's voice and stay true to the original narrative while maintaining historical accuracy. General information on major organizations, significant historical events and people, geographical locations, religious and cultural terms, and foreign-language words and expressions that will help give context to the events described in the text can be found in the glossary beginning on page 161.

Introduction

Jack (Jankiel) Klajman was born April 22, 1931, into what he describes in his memoir as a "typical Jewish family in Warsaw." As the second youngest of five children living in a small apartment in the heart of Warsaw's Jewish section, his world would be shattered in 1939 with the German invasion of Poland. Out of the approximately one million Jewish children in Poland at the start of the war, Jack would be one of only about five thousand to survive the war. His story of survival, marked by extraordinary courage, heartbreak, resilience, luck and trauma, is significant not only because it spotlights the perspective of a child able to survive through smuggling food and other essential items into the Warsaw ghetto before going into hiding but also because Jack represents the 0.05 per cent of Polish Jewish children who somehow managed to survive the Nazi genocide.

As a working-class family living in the heart of Jewish Warsaw, the Klajmans were characteristic of the broader Warsaw Jewish community. Jack's father operated a fur workshop in the winter and a small shoe factory in spring and summer, while his mother kept the books and managed a booth at the market, selling sandals to farmers on

NOTE: This introduction was adapted from Avinoam Patt's *The Jewish Heroes of Warsaw: The Afterlife of the Revolt* (Wayne State University Press, 2021), with permission of Wayne State University Press.

market days. These skills in trading and retail would serve Jack well when he was forced to smuggle, negotiate and trade to survive. The Klajman family was part of the thriving Jewish community in the heart of Warsaw, which in 1939 was the second largest Jewish city in the world; only New York had a larger Jewish population at the time. (Warsaw's population of 337,000 Jews in 1914 was equal to the entire Jewish population of France.[1]) Warsaw had turned into a major Jewish centre over the course of the nineteenth century as rapid industrialization and urbanization attracted a modernizing Jewish population. Warsaw became the capital of an independent Poland after World War I, and Jews from parts of the newly created Poland that had formerly been part of the Austro-Hungarian Empire (like Galicia) or the Russian Empire streamed toward the new capital, eager to partake in the economic, educational and political opportunities it offered. As the population of Warsaw grew in the interwar period, so did its Jewish population, to 368,394 in 1938.[2]

Although Jews were allowed to live wherever they wished in Warsaw, the northwestern section of the city, especially Muranów, became the cultural, economic, social and religious centre of Jewish life. In 1938, Jews comprised no less than 90.5 per cent of all inhabitants in the Muranów district alone.[3] While Jews were increasingly dispersed around the city, the centre of Jewish Warsaw remained around the Nalewki, a hectic thoroughfare awash with shouting peddlers, artisans, the unemployed and those employed in legal and illegal ways. The Klajman family lived at 14 Wołyńska Street, just around the corner from the Nalewki.

Over the course of the 1930s, despite promises of democratic freedom and protection of minority rights in interwar Poland, the situation of the Jews in Poland (and of Jewish Warsaw) deteriorated, as public expressions of hostility against Jews increased, along with calls for the emigration of Jews from Poland, the establishment of separate seating for Jews (ghetto benches) in the universities, and a general increase in violence against Jews.

As Jack recalls in the memoir, by August 1939, Poles (Jews and non-Jews alike) began to prepare for what seemed like an imminent German invasion. With the outbreak of war on September 1, 1939, all of Warsaw's residents suffered from the indiscriminate bombing of the Luftwaffe. An American Jewish Joint Distribution Committee (AJDC) report in Warsaw estimated that twenty thousand Jews were killed in the first month of the war, with seven thousand Jews killed in Warsaw alone in September 1939.[4] Jack describes those first terrifying days of the war:

Several bombers swooped over our neighbourhood — an area of about fifteen condensed blocks. The bombs dropped were devastating — lighting the area up in fire and smoke. [...]

We ran carefully from house to house, dodging the Luftwaffe's bombs. Our neighbourhood was engulfed in flames, the blaze coming from many buildings. And once the fire had burned all it could, what was left of the buildings came crashing to the ground.

The bombing campaign destroyed the Klajmans' property and all of their possessions, leaving the family with only the clothes on their backs. Jack's depiction provides a sense of the chaos, horror and panic experienced during the German invasion, and this was only the beginning of the nightmare for Polish Jews.

While some Jews managed to flee to the East (adult men of military age like Jack's oldest brother, Getzel, were especially afraid of capture) the majority remained in Warsaw as the German occupation began. By early 1940, the Jewish population of Warsaw swelled to some 400,000 as Jews from areas annexed to the Reich were deported to the *Generalgouvernement*, and refugees crowded into Warsaw.[5] This only further compounded the scarcity of housing, food and medical supplies in the city. Displaced from their home, the Klajman family eventually managed to find a small place at 64 Miła Street (inside the area that would become the ghetto), where the entire family was forced to crowd together inside a one-room apartment.

By September 28, 1939, the siege of Warsaw was over, with fully one-quarter of the city's buildings having been destroyed and as many as fifty thousand citizens killed or injured.[6] Jews quickly experienced the changing dynamics of Polish society under German occupation. In addition to the process of social isolation and extreme persecution that unfolded in Warsaw and throughout occupied Poland, the official establishment of the *Generalgouvernement* under the leadership of Hans Frank soon subjected Jews to special decrees that limited them to two thousand złotys in cash, blocked their access to bank accounts, limited their use of trains and public transport, instituted the "Aryanization" of Jewish businesses and subjected Jews between the ages of fourteen and sixty to random seizure for forced labour.[7] By December 1, 1939, Hans Frank had decreed that all Jews over the age of ten residing in the *Generalgouvernement* must wear white armbands with a Star of David on the right sleeve of their clothing.[8] Adam Czerniaków was named head of the Jewish Council (or Judenrat), which attempted to intervene with the German authorities to prevent random kidnappings of Jews seized in the streets for forced labour, who endured terrible torture in the process. Instead, the German authorities obligated the Judenrat to provide two thousand workers for the Germans daily, even as random seizures continued.[9] For the Jewish public in Warsaw, this seemed to make the Judenrat complicit in German policy, eventually opening a space for an alternative underground leadership in Jewish Warsaw to emerge as the Nazi policy of persecution continued and increased.

German authorities established the first ghetto in Poland in Piotrków Trybunalski in October 1939, but it would take another year for the ghetto in Warsaw to be sealed. Jewish leaders in Warsaw argued (correctly) that imprisoning the Jewish population in a ghetto would lead to the rapid spread of disease. Nonetheless, on March 27, 1940, the Warsaw Judenrat received orders to begin the construction of walls around a "plague-infected area" in the Jewish residential section of Warsaw; by the beginning of June, at least twenty sections of the wall had been erected, and in August 1940, German authorities issued an official announcement that the city would be divided into German, Polish and Jewish quarters.[10] On Yom Kippur 1940 (October 12), the Jews of Warsaw were informed by announcements made over street megaphones that all Jews in the city would be required to move into the ghetto by the end of the month.[11] On November 15, 1940, German authorities ordered the Warsaw ghetto sealed off, creating the largest ghetto in both area and population in Poland. Over 350,000 Jews, approximately 30 per cent of the city's population, were confined to about 2.4 per cent of Warsaw's total area. Over 120,000 additional refugees would later be sent to the ghetto, bringing the total population of the ghetto to nearly 500,000.[12]

The results of crowding nearly half a million people into such a tiny area were catastrophic. Mass starvation and widespread disease led to a staggering death rate within the ghetto. Approximately 43,000 ghetto inhabitants (10 per cent of the ghetto population) died over the course of 1941, marking the time before the initiation of the mass deportation as the period of "gradual extermination."[13] As Jack recalls, "by early 1941.... it became common to see men, women and especially children dying in the streets. Corpses were dragged off the sidewalks for mass burials of fifty at a time." While many other children took to begging in the streets, Jack realized that this would only stave off death temporarily for him and his family:

Closed off from the outside world, most children took to the ghetto streets to beg for food. But there were thousands of children and precious little food. I realized this tactic was sure to lead to starvation and saw only one solution; somehow, I had to leave the ghetto to get food.

Smuggling would become a critical lifeline for the family, at least for a limited time.

The Judenrat was forced to take over responsibility for basic nutrition, public health (and prevention of the spread of disease), sanitation (removal of garbage from the ghetto), maintaining public order (police and firefighting), housing and registering the ghetto inhabitants. They not only had to administer daily affairs but also had to ensure compliance with German regulations. Under the extreme conditions created in the ghetto — the food crisis, the economic crisis, the housing crisis, the public health crisis and the refugee crisis — the work of social welfare organizations to address all of these issues became critical. But even with the efforts of the Jewish Council, the Jewish self-help organization and the house committees established in almost every apartment bloc, the Germans continued to starve the Jewish population; without enough food, Jews continued to die on the streets from hunger and disease.

The house committees were centred in the inner courtyards of the large apartment buildings in the Jewish quarter, which seemed to offer more security from the dangers of the street. As historian Samuel Kassow suggests, "the house committees quickly became the basis of public life in the Warsaw ghetto," providing communal kitchens, childcare, shelter for the sick and a safe place for social interaction.[14] In addition to maintaining social welfare organizations in the ghetto, Jewish organizations tried to maintain an active cultural, educational and religious life, despite the abominable conditions and a German ban on most educational activities. Nonetheless, in reading Jack's memoir, we see a boy whose schooling was cut off at the age of eight, who quickly had to adapt to the catastrophic situation of life in the ghetto and use his wits, quick thinking and "street smarts" to survive. Despite the best efforts of social and cultural organizations in the ghetto, children like Jack were burying family members and stepping over dead bodies in the streets when they should have been in school.

The social welfare activist and historian Emanuel Ringelblum organized the Oneg Shabbes underground archive in the ghetto around the networks of the Jewish self-help organization, using the refugee points, soup kitchens, house committees and underground schools to provide the information, documents and testimonies for the archive. After July 22, 1942, the archive documented what became known as the Great Deportation, collecting posters that had called on Jews to assemble for transport and the desperate appeals from those waiting to board deportation trains (to Treblinka), which were crammed into milk cans, as well as the later posters calling for armed resistance in 1943. The materials collected by the archive also demonstrate that despite the hardships of life in the ghetto, Jews believed they could maintain elements of communal life under such circumstances, holding out hope for survival until the war ended.

Ringelblum also singled out the role of the little smugglers (as depicted by Jack in this memoir), who would play such a crucial role in risking their lives to bring food into the ghetto and thus help keep their families alive. As Ringelblum described in his diary:

Smuggling began at the very moment that the Jewish area of residence was established; its inhabitants were forced to live on 180 grams of bread a day, 220 grams of sugar a month, 1 kg. of jam and 1 kg. of honey, etc. It was calculated that the officially supplied rations did not cover even 10 per cent of the normal requirements. If one had wanted really to restrict oneself to the official rations then the entire population of the ghetto would have had to die of hunger in a very short time....[15]

As noted by Jack, smuggling was extremely dangerous, and children were often captured, beaten and shot to death crawling over, under and through the ghetto walls. And yet, it was often the only way to keep a family alive as the official rations were designed to starve Jews to death. Jack describes what it was like for the children who became smugglers:

We were resourceful, using whatever means available to get out of the ghetto. We were small, which meant we were often able to get through small drainage holes in the bottom of the walls or other holes that adults made for us. We also broke through ourselves by chipping away one brick at a time until there was a hole big enough to just squeeze through. Often, the German guards and Polish police would find our holes and fill them in, so we would always be looking to punch out new ones to stay one step ahead of them.

When it wasn't possible to go through the wall, we went over it. This was the more difficult way because we had to scale all the brick and then manoeuvre across the crushed glass cemented at the top. We put thick rags over the glass so we could stay at the top for a few moments before jumping down. Even after getting to the other side, we were only partway to safety. With guards buzzing around the wall and all its entrances, there was no assurance we'd get away from the wall undetected.

The food and other items brought into the ghetto by little smugglers like Jack became invaluable to life in the ghetto.

As Jack would note in his recollections: "I often had more guts than brains during those smuggling days. I also had a lot of luck." Caught numerous times, he somehow managed to stay alive. Nonetheless, by the time Jack turned eleven, he was an orphan, having lost both his parents to starvation and disease by the fall of 1941. Jack had to continue sneaking in and out of the ghetto to support his siblings who remained in the ghetto, all the while avoiding the informers eager to turn over Jews just for a small reward.

Meanwhile, as the cumulative process of extreme hunger, daily terror and continued oppression led to the polarization and atomization of Jewish Warsaw, in the spring of 1942 the Germans had begun to implement the so-called Final Solution in the *Generalgouvernement* within the framework of Operation Reinhard. The Germans were sending transports of Jews from the ghettos of Poland to the newly constructed killing centres at Belzec (where killing began in March 1942), Sobibor (May 1942) and Treblinka (July 1942). The ghetto diarist Chaim Kaplan, who had served as a principal of a Hebrew elementary school in Warsaw for decades, recorded the sense of bewilderment and confusion on the part of the ghetto's population as the liquidation approached, along with the dashed hopes of survival and the terror of deportation: "There is an instinctive feeling that some terrible catastrophe is drawing near for the Warsaw ghetto, though no one can determine its time or details" (June 20, 1942).[16] Jack would find himself trapped inside the ghetto on the day the Great Deportation began, managing to hide in an attic with friends who were also smugglers.

On July 22, 1942, the Great Deportation from the Warsaw ghetto to Treblinka began, as German SS and police authorities initiated the process that led to the deportation of approximately 275,000–300,000 Jews from the ghetto by September 12, 1942. Adam Czerniaków, chairman of the Warsaw ghetto Judenrat, died by suicide on July 23, 1942, rather than comply with the deportation order, writing in his final note, "They are demanding that I kill the children of my people with my own hands. There is nothing for me to do but die."[17] The *Umschlagplatz*, on the northern edge of the ghetto, became the scene of indescribable suffering, as Jews rounded up in the ghetto waited to board the trains that would take them to Treblinka. Jack managed to survive once again, escaping from the ghetto at the end of July to be reunited with his brother Eli on the "Aryan" side of Warsaw.

By late September 1942, Jewish forced labourers working in work-shops comprised the ghetto population of approximately 55,000. As knowledge of the true nature of Treblinka became widespread in the ghetto, some began to seek ways to remove family members to the "Aryan" side of Warsaw, while others began to build hiding places and bunkers inside the ghetto.[18] In the words of Ringelblum, while the adult generation continued to worry about survival and about the possibility of continuing life, it was

the youth — the best, the most beautiful, the noblest element that the Jewish people possessed — [who] spoke and thought only about an honorable death. They did not think about surviving the war, they did not arrange "Aryan" Papers, they did not get apartments on the other side. Their only worry was about the most honorable death, the kind of death that a two-thousand-year-old people deserves.[19]

In conjunction with the six-month anniversary of the Great Deportation, the Jewish Fighting Organization (ŻOB), also known as the
Jewish Combat Organization, which had only managed to come together in the aftermath of the July 1942 deportations, planned a retaliation against the Jewish police for their role in those roundups,
calling on the remaining Jews of Warsaw:

*Jewish masses, the hour is drawing near. You must be prepared to resist,
not give yourselves up to slaughter like sheep. Not a single Jew should
go to the railroad cars. Those who are unable to put up active resistance
should resist passively, meaning go into hiding.... Our motto should
be:* All are ready to die as human beings.[20]

Before their planned retaliation could take place, however, on January
18, 1943, the Nazis surprised the Jewish fighters, entering the ghetto
and deporting 6,500 Jews. With the limited supply of weapons they
had already managed to smuggle into the ghetto, Jewish fighters fired
upon German troops during a roundup, leading the soldiers to retreat. The ghetto fighters learned valuable lessons from this first con-
flict, which they applied to the next stage of the resistance.

Even after the Great Deportation, Żegota, the Council for Aid to
Jews affiliated with the Polish government-in-exile, remained especially concerned with the plight of Jewish children. Following the liq-
uidations of summer 1942, a number of parents were able to get their
children to the "Aryan" side of Warsaw by paying large sums to Polish
smugglers and police, with the aid of the Polish underground and
Żegota. Irena Sendler ("Jolanta") assisted in smuggling hundreds of
children from the ghetto and is probably the most well known of the
rescuers associated with the organization. Jan Dobraczyński, director
of the Child Care Section in the Social Aid Department of the Warsaw Municipality, helped to place Jewish children in Polish orphanages and monasteries.[21] In other cases, Jews were sheltered outside
the ghetto by friendly non-Jewish Poles, many of whom would later

be recognized as Righteous Among the Nations by Yad Vashem. Jack and his younger brother Eli, orphaned and alone outside the ghetto by this time, lived as nomads sleeping where they could, hoping to avoid soldiers, police and informers who would turn them in for a bag of sugar. The persistence of Polish antisemitism made it almost impossible for Jews who managed to escape from the ghetto to survive on the outside.

Following the January 1943 uprising, in which the ŻOB gained its first experience in battle against German forces and learned important lessons about avoiding direct combat with the superior firepower of the German army, a period of relative quiet ensued in the ghetto. German officials debated the proper course of action, with some arguing for complete liquidation of the ghetto and others lobbying for the continued use or transfer of the workers in the armaments, leather and textile factories in Warsaw to other parts of the *General-gouvernement*. The remaining Jews in the ghetto had been convinced that the time had come for armed resistance as the course of last resort, refusing to believe German assurances that transfer to labour camps at Trawniki or Poniatowa would enable them to survive until the end of the war.[22] The remaining population also devoted itself to preparing bunkers in the ghetto; as one survivor noted: "one can say without exaggeration that the entire population, from the young to the old, was engaged in preparing hiding places…. No one thought of willingly going to Treblinka. The survivors prepared everything necessary for remaining in hiding for months."[23]

As the historian Havi Dreifuss emphasizes, one of the lessons learned from witnesses to the January resistance was that armed resistance was not the only way to "fight back." Some realized that it would be even better to engage in passive resistance and go into hiding.[24] At the same time, the ŻOB focused on acquiring funds to purchase arms, while also working to purge any dangerous collaborators from their midst.[25]

In the fall of 1942 and beginning of 1943, Jack and Eli survived on the streets of Warsaw, scraping by with whatever food they could get their hands on and seeking safe places to sleep. Smuggling still generated more money than begging, and Jack made occasional forays into the ghetto where he learned that most of his comrades had been deported to Treblinka. In the spring of 1943, Jack continued to sneak in and out of the ghetto, smuggling whatever supplies were needed for the surviving population, while coming into closer contact with members of the ŻOB. This was how Jack would find himself inside the ghetto when the Warsaw Ghetto Uprising began, delivering Passover treats to his smuggling friends, now resistance fighters readying themselves for the imminent attack.

The final liquidation of the Warsaw ghetto began on Passover Eve, April 19, 1943. Approximately two thousand German soldiers (including SS troops, German police and army soldiers), commanded by SS Senior Colonel Ferdinand von Sammern-Frankenegg, entered the ghetto early that morning. While the German forces were surprised by the size of the Jewish resistance, the ŻOB and the Jewish fighters were prepared for the German liquidation. The day before, on April 18, 1943, the ghetto had begun to receive reports that German forces were massing outside the ghetto. Accordingly, Jews began to gather in their bunkers that night, and ŻOB fighters, prepared to encounter the German forces in their combat units, mobilized by 2:15 a.m.[26]

Jack recalls in his memoir how he, as a young boy, witnessed this preparation through his contact with smugglers and describes his enthusiasm to help in any way he could, including as a messenger for the ŻOB fighters. Although he never came into contact with Mordecai Anielewicz, the commander of the ŻOB, Jack was close with prominent smugglers in the ghetto, who played a vital role in supplying arms and food to the ghetto fighters. After the first day of fighting in the ghetto, Mordecai Anielewicz managed to send a letter to his comrade Yitzhak Zuckerman outside the ghetto (which would become known as the "last letter of the Warsaw Ghetto Uprising's commander") via the Jewish cemetery. As Anielewicz concluded: "The main thing: the dream of my life was realized. I have been privileged to witness Jewish Self-Defense in the Ghetto in all of its greatness and majesty."[27]

The Jewish underground both inside and outside the ghetto continued to relay reports as the uprising unfolded, detailing the final days of the ghetto. The fighters managed to initially repel German attempts to liquidate the ghetto and employed guerrilla tactics that forced the Germans to proceed in house-to-house fighting, sustaining high numbers of casualties. Soon, the Germans shifted tactics to begin burning down houses and apartment blocs, and dwindling supplies of ammunition led to a weakening of the resistance. In truth, there were just a few hundred armed Jewish fighters in the ghetto; the vast majority of the population resisted the German liquidation efforts by hiding out in bunkers underneath the ghetto, just as Jack did. By the tenth day of the uprising, it was clear to some members of the ŻOB (who rejected the idea of certain death and symbolic sacrifice in the ghetto) that a way out of the ghetto should be found for those remaining fighters who wanted to escape. The fighters had prepared to do battle with the German soldiers and their collaborators, but they were not prepared to do battle with the fires that destroyed every building in the ghetto. The Germans also used these fires to force Jews out of the bunkers underground, just as Jack describes the predicament faced by the group of over a hundred Jews he sheltered with during the revolt:

Rather than coming in after us, the Germans used the threat of fire to flush us out. I think they stayed back because they feared we had guns or that the bunker was booby-trapped with explosives…. People were shaking with fear. Women and children were crying and screaming.

After emerging from the bunker, Jack's quick thinking and bravery — and luck — enabled him to escape and evade detection, but such was not the case for most of the Jews who remained in the ghetto. By the end of the first week of the "ghetto operation," SS General Jurgen Stroop reported increasing success apprehending the remaining ghetto population, including those Jews caught hiding in bunkers, those burned out of buildings in the ghetto and those discovered in the sewers under the city.[28] On the twentieth day of fighting, on May 8, 1943, the central command bunker of the ŻOB at 18 Miła Street was discovered, and the Germans began to pipe poison gas into the bunker to flush the Jewish fighters out. Most of those in the group, including Anielewicz, took cyanide pills when they could no longer fight off the gas, and a group of approximately forty ghetto fighters managed to escape via the sewers. Like the ghetto fighters, Jack also managed to flee from the ghetto through the sewers, led by a Polish sewage worker who had been bribed to guide his group under the streets of Warsaw through filth and muck to the "Aryan" side.

On May 16, 1943, Stroop celebrated the final liquidation of the ghetto by ordering the destruction of the Great Synagogue on Tłomackie Street. After a month of fighting, the ghetto was in ruins. Stroop reported the capture of over 56,065 Jews and the destruction of 631 bunkers, killing 7,000 Jews in the uprising and deporting another 7,000 to Treblinka.[29] Other captured Jews were sent to Majdanek and forced labour camps at Trawniki and Poniatowa. The Warsaw Ghetto Uprising, as the first mass revolt in a major city in Nazi-occupied Europe, became a symbol of Jewish resistance to Nazi oppression, inspiring similar revolts in Białystok and Minsk, as well as uprisings in Treblinka and Sobibor later in 1943.

Once the revolt had been suppressed, out of a peak population of 500,000 Jews in Warsaw, perhaps 20,000 Jews remained. One year after the revolt, in May 1944, the Jewish National Committee, the largest underground Jewish relief organization in Warsaw, had over a hundred cells, which cared for five thousand Jews. Furthermore, the Jewish National Committee also worked to rescue Jews who remained in concentration camps and was active in producing false identification cards, birth certificates, residence permits, work permits and more for scores of Jews living in hiding. Almost every Jew who managed to survive in hiding needed the help of an aid organization, Żegota, righteous gentiles or the Jewish underground. Jack managed to stay alive with the assistance of a kind Polish woman, Mrs. Lodzia. During this time, Jack managed to join up with the cigarette sellers of Three Crosses Square, continuing his ability to smuggle and trade to stay alive. This connection also enabled him to obtain false papers under the pseudonym he had adopted, Janek Jankowski. And indeed, the Jewish National Committee worked to provide false papers for the boys surviving as cigarette sellers in Three Crosses Square, providing documents that could help evade capture, arrest and certain death.[30]

Many Jews who had remained in hiding in Warsaw emerged to join the failed Warsaw Uprising in August 1944. The Warsaw Uprising began on August 1, 1944, and lasted sixty days, until it was brutally suppressed by the Germans at the beginning of October. The uprising was launched by the Polish Home Army (Armia Krajowa), the largest Polish resistance organization, based on orders from the London-based Polish government-in-exile. The Home Army's goal was to take control of Warsaw from the Germans before the Soviet army reached the city, with the Red Army appearing on the other side of the Wisła River not far from Warsaw. In all, about 16,000–20,000 Polish fighters were either killed or went missing and 7,000 were wounded. Approximately 150,000 civilians were also killed, including several thousand Jews who had hidden with Poles in Warsaw after the ghetto was liquidated in May 1943.[31]

Soviet troops liberated Warsaw on January 17, 1945, after failing to intervene as the Germans crushed the revolt, revealing a completely devastated Warsaw. The city's population had dwindled to 174,000 people, and according to Polish data approximately 11,500 of these survivors were Jews.[32] Liberated Jews searched for family and friends, looking for news of who had survived and how most had perished. Once Jack realized that he was the only member of his family who had managed to survive, he resolved to leave as soon as he could: "Warsaw had brought me nothing but heartache and sorrow, and I knew my best chance at happiness would be far away from it." He was advised by a group of Jewish soldiers serving with the Red Army to travel to Lublin, where what was left of the Polish Jewish community had begun to organize after its liberation in July 1944.

Reports emerging from Lublin by January 1945 did not paint a promising portrait of the Jewish situation. The Jewish population continued to be ravaged by disease and malnutrition, and the public kitchens could not provide sufficient food to satisfy the minimum needs of the hungry and the needy. Jews had considerable difficulties regaining possession of lost property, both individually and communally. While many Jewish orphans were wandering the streets of Lublin, the Jewish orphanage there continued to be occupied by Polish institutions. The surviving Jewish population faced continuing violence and hostility from the local population, with Jews facing both physical and verbal attacks, as well as vandalism to their homes and shops.[33] An estimated 10–12 per cent of the Jewish population in Poland in 1945 was between the ages of fifteen and twenty.[34]

The first recourse for many young Jewish survivors in Poland after the war was to turn to the newly formed local Jewish committees, seeking answers to their most pressing needs, including food, shelter, health and security, before they could turn to the larger questions of how and where to continue their lives. For many survivors in postwar Poland, including thousands who would be repatriated from the Soviet Union, where they had managed to survive the war, the continuing antisemitism and threat of violence led them to the conclusion that there was no future for them in Poland. Over the course of 1945 and 1946, the movement of surviving Jews departing Poland would continue to grow, with some 110,000 Polish Jews choosing to depart Poland with the Bricha, the semi-organized movement of escape to Palestine, even before the Kielce pogrom of July 1946; of these, some 33,600 were youth organized by Zionist groups in kibbutzim.[35]

Jack's journey to the American zone of Germany via Prague paralleled a route taken by many surviving youth eager to escape from Poland. Many would end up in pre-state Israel, while others would make their way to the United States, Canada, Australia, South America and elsewhere. Jack was part of a small group of Jewish orphans sponsored by the Central British Fund for German Jewry. Eventually he would make his way to Canada, where fittingly he would return to the family fur business.

When we take into account that the Nazis murdered 1.5 million Jewish children during the war, it is perhaps unsurprising that the few surviving children would become the focus of the hopes and dreams of the Jewish future in the aftermath of the war. As an eyewitness to the destruction of Jewish Warsaw, Jack Klajman's account is remarkable; as one of so few Polish Jewish children to survive the war, this story of survival is not only a tragic tale of courage, resilience and profound loss, it is nothing short of miraculous.

Avinoam J. Patt, PhD
Doris and Simon Konover Chair of Judaic Studies
Director, Center for Judaic Studies and Contemporary Jewish Life
University of Connecticut
2023

NOTES

1 Antony Polonsky, s.v. "Warsaw," *The YIVO Encyclopedia of Jews in Eastern Europe,* http://www.yivoencyclopedia.org/article.aspx/Warsaw

2 Barbara Engelking and Jacek Leociak, *The Warsaw Ghetto: A Guide to the Perished City* (New Haven: Yale University Press, 2009), 15.

3 See Michael Meng, *Shattered Spaces: Encountering Jewish Ruins in Postwar Germany and Poland* (Cambridge: Harvard University Press, 2011).

4 Cited in Alexandra Garbarini, Emil Kerenji, Jan Lambertz and Avinoam Patt, *Jewish Responses to Persecution, Volume II, 1938–1940* (Washington, DC: USHMM/AltaMira Press, 2011), 121.

5 Engelking and Leociak, 47–48.

6 Samuel Kassow, *Who Will Write Our History: Emanuel Ringelblum, the Warsaw Ghetto, and the Oyneg Shabes Archive* (Bloomington: Indiana University Press, 2007), 106.

7 Kassow, 106–107.

8 Saul Friedlander, *The Years of Extermination: Nazi Germany and the Jews, 1939–1945* (New York: Harper Perennial, 2008), 38.

9 Szmul Zygielbojm, "Kidnapping for Labor," no date (circa December 1939), Zygielbojm-bukh (New York: Farlag "Unzer Tsayt," 1947), 142–50 (translated from Yiddish).

10 See in Israel Gutman, *The Jews of Warsaw, 1939–1943: Ghetto, Underground, Revolt* (Bloomington: Indiana University Press, 1982), 50–51.

11 See Engelking and Leociak, 642; Chaim Kaplan, *Scroll of Agony: The Warsaw Diary of Chaim A. Kaplan*, trans. Abraham I. Katsh (Bloomington: Indiana University Press, 1999), 208.

12 See Gutman, *The Jews of Warsaw*, 60–61. It is impossible to provide accurate numbers of Jewish refugees and ghetto inhabitants in Warsaw for this chaotic period. Israel Gutman (*The Jews of Warsaw*, 63) cites 130,000 Jewish refugees in Warsaw by April 1941, while Yehuda Bauer (*American Jewry*, 69) estimates the number of Jewish refugees in the city at 150,000 after September 1940. Barbara Engelking and Jacek Leociak (49) estimate the peak number of inhabitants of the Warsaw ghetto at 460,000 in March 1941 (15,000 more than Gutman's number for the same month) and quote Nazi documents that put the number as high as 490,000.

13 Gutman, 64.

14 Kassow, 121. By April 1940, 778 such committees had been set up in the Jewish quarter of the city, and eventually this number would reach 1,518, covering more than 2,000 houses. See Gutman, *The Jews of Warsaw*, 45–47; Saul Friedländer, *The Years of Extermination: Nazi Germany and the Jews, 1939–1945*, volume 2 (New York: HarperCollins, 2007), 148.

15 Emanuel Ringelblum quoted in Yitzhak Arad, ed., *Documents on the Holocaust: Selected Sources on the Destruction of the Jews of Germany and Austria, Poland, and the Soviet Union* (Jerusalem: Yad Vashem, 1987), 228–229.

16 See as recorded in http://www.jewishgen.org/yizkor/terrible_choice/ter003.html (accessed February 2023); Kaplan, *Scroll of Agony*.

17 For a detailed account of the Deportation, see Engelking and Leociak, 698–730. Havi Dreifuss in *Geto Varsha — HaSof: April 1942–June 1943 (Warsaw Ghetto — The End)* (Jerusalem: Yad Vashem, 2017) suggests it is possible there was another note which was not publicized where Czerniaków advised the Jewish public to take his actions as a sign and draw their own conclusions. See Dreifuss, 150.

18 Dreifuss, *Geto Varsha*, 310.

19 Ringelblum, *Ksovim*, vol. 2, 148–149; Kassow, 371.

20 Call to Resistance by the Jewish Fighting Organization in the Warsaw Ghetto, January 1943, *Archiwum Zydowskiego Instytutu Historycznego w Polsce* (Archives of the Jewish Historical Institute in Poland), ARII/333. (cited in Gutman, 305). See also Joseph Kermish, *Rescue Attempts during the Holocaust, Proceedings of the Second Yad Vashem International Historical Conference*, ed. Yisrael Gutman and Efraim Zuroff (Jerusalem: Yad Vashem, 1977), 589.

21 Kermish, 367–398.

22 Gutman, 334.

23 Gutman, 351.

24 Dreifuss, *Geto Varsha*, 333.

25 Gutman, 340.

26 See, for example, the reports of Tuvia Borzykowski, *Between Tumbling Walls* (Israel: HaKibbutz HaMeuchad Publishing House, 1976) and Marek Edelman, *The Ghetto Fights* (London: Bookmarks, 2014); also Gutman, 367–368.

27 This translation is based on the Hebrew transcript reproduced in *Sefer Milhamot HaGetaot*, 158. As Dreifuss explains, subsequent versions of the "final letter" include additions by Berman not part of the original letter.

28 Stroop Report, 197.

29 See Stroop Report in *Revolt amid the Darkness* (Washington: USHMM, 1993), 199.

30 "Commemoration of Cigarette Sellers of Three Crosses Square in Warsaw," February 23, 2021, https://warszawa.jewish.org.pl/2021/02/commemoration-of-cigarette-sellers-of-three-crosses-square-in-warsaw/

31 See the detailed account in Joshua D. Zimmerman, *The Polish Underground and Jews* (New York: Cambridge University Press, 2015), statistics on page 408.

32 See "Warsaw," USHMM *Holocaust Encyclopedia*, https://encyclopedia.ushmm.org/content/en/article/warsaw.

33 "The Situation of the Jews in Liberated Poland," Report from Jerusalem, Jewish Agency, March 23, 1945, Ha'apalah Project, Haganah Archives (Gordonia/Maccabi Tzair Archives, 3/111). The document is a summary of reports from Lublin in January 1945.

34 David Engel, *Bein Shichrur Li-Verichah: Nitzulei HaShoah Be-Polin Ve-Hamavak al Hanhagatam, 1944–1946* (Tel Aviv: Am Oved Press, 1996), 203–204, n. 221. On the basis of registrations from Jewish communities where the age of registrants was noted, he concludes that it would seem that the proportion of youth to the general Jewish population was 10–12 per cent.

35 Table from Yochanan Cohen, *Ovrim kol Gvul: HaBrichah, Polin 1945–1946* (Tel Aviv: Zemorah-Bitan, 1995), 469.

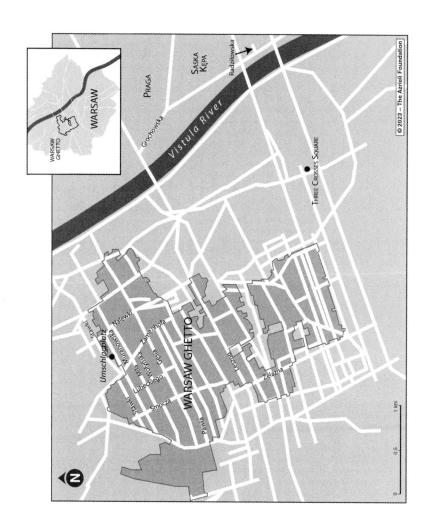

I thank my son Ed for his countless hours of writing, editing and researching, which made this book possible.

Preface

This book chronicles the story of my experiences in Warsaw during World War II. I have recounted my story to the best of my recollection and in my own words, writing from the perspective of a young child, as I was only eight years old when the war began.

I first thought about writing this book in 1948 and started many drafts over the years. But each time I found that it was too difficult to relive all the painful memories. I would break down in tears as soon as I would get a few lines on paper. This time, perhaps because I am getting on in years, I refused to let any emotions prevent me from writing.

Once I focused on tapping my memory bank, all the experiences came flooding out in detail. They had been locked deeply away in the back of my mind for decades, only surfacing occasionally in the middle of the night when I woke up in a cold sweat because of vivid nightmares in which Germans are trying to kill me. It seems a person can bury the past but cannot get rid of it.

I am proud that I have documented my experiences and made my contribution to the historical record. My story is not a happy one, but it is important that I tell it. My wife and four children should know what I saw and lived through. I dedicate this book to them.

As Our City Burns

On April 22, 1931, I was born into a typical Jewish family in Warsaw. My parents named me Jankiel (Jack in English). I was the second youngest of five children.

We lived in a small apartment in the heart of the city's Jewish section — at 14 Wołyńska Street. My father, Mendel, was a tradesman who worked at home. During the fall and winter, he made fur accessories for cloth-coat manufacturers. In Poland in the 1930s, men displayed their affluence by wearing large outer collars of fur. Women who considered themselves prosperous wore mink collars and a muff to match to feel elegant. The popularity of fur meant there was plenty of work from garment shops to keep my father busy.

In the spring and summer, my father converted his fur workshop into a small shoe factory, where he made children's and women's sandals. These were then sold to local shoe stores.

My father was the labourer, and my mother, Ita, ran the business. She would keep the books and take care of all the sales to manufacturers and shopkeepers. She even started a small retail operation. In the warmer months, farmers from the countryside would come to town once a week to sell their produce, and my mother would set up a booth at these markets to sell sandals to the farmers. It was always busy, so I would help her by being on guard for potential thieves.

My mother considered her mother to be the role model for all of us to follow. When my mom was four years old, her father died from an illness, and her mother was left to raise three children alone. She bought a piece of land about thirty kilometres outside of Warsaw, where she ran a farm and had an orchard for growing apples, pears and cherries.

Grandma used to refer to herself as a city girl turned farmer. "The fresh air and the healthy fruit and vegetables will keep you alive until you are a hundred years old," she would say. In her seventies, she still loved to live and work at the farm. She was incredibly generous. She would ride in on her horse-and-buggy to bring us bags full of potatoes, turnips and cabbages, which we would store for the winter.

We had a close family, and I never had any problems with any of my four siblings. Getzel (Gedalje) was the oldest — eighteen when the war began — and Brenda (Broncha) was two years younger. There was then a gap of five years between her and Menashe; I was eight, and my little brother Eli was six.

I also had another brother I never met, who had been born a year after Brenda, but he died at the age of one. My mom and dad had been invited to an engagement party and left the children with a babysitter. The woman watching them was incompetent and let the little boy wander unguarded. He fell and struck his head on the corner of a wooden table. The sitter didn't tell my mother about the incident, thinking it wasn't serious. Later that night, when the boy didn't look good and ran a high fever, my mom had no idea what had happened. My parents rushed him to the hospital, where he died the next day. Apparently, he had suffered a severe concussion that led to some major internal bleeding. The babysitter's carelessness cost my brother his life.

Our parents did their best to give us a happy childhood, and we loved and respected them for it. I still remember some of our more enjoyable moments. For instance, each Passover we would all get new clothes and have a large feast, which considering our lack of wealth was quite a big deal. In our neighbourhood, anyone who could afford to eat three meals a day was considered well off.

My mother's intense commitment to her religious faith shaped my childhood. She knew pages of Jewish prayers by heart. When I was four years old, she began educating me in how to read the Talmud. Although she was extremely knowledgeable about Judaism, she couldn't read or write Polish. She did, however, speak enough of it to get by as a salesperson.

My best friend when I was young was a blue-eyed, blond-haired little girl named Irka Ksrigika. She lived just down the street from us at 4 Wołyńska Street — the second-last house before Ludwika Zamenhofa Street.

My first memories of Irka are from the age of seven, when we were in Grade 1. In the building where my family lived, many of the adults would get together to stage plays for Saturday afternoon entertainment. Irka and I would dance together at these events to the amusement of all the people in our building.

During the week, I always stopped off at her place so we could walk together to our primary school, which was just around the corner from where we lived. Both Irka and I were at the head of our class — she had the highest grade of the girls, while I was first among the boys.

Unfortunately, neither of us would be able to experience Grade 2.

~

Our Nazi nightmare began late in the summer of 1939. In late August, people would gather in the streets to talk about what seemed to be an imminent German invasion. Grocery store owners were hoarding food and charged outrageous amounts for what they made available. People in our Jewish neighbourhood were particularly vulnerable to those price increases.

On September 1, the war began when Germany invaded Poland. I was only eight years old at the time, but it is a day I will never forget.

Late that afternoon, each member of our family was in line at the local bakery. We were preparing for a big family dinner. The bakery was only selling one loaf per person, so each of us had to stand in line to buy a loaf. We had just returned home when we heard planes flying over the city. At first, we hoped they might be Polish, but that thought didn't last long. Several bombers swooped over our neighbourhood — an area of about fifteen condensed blocks. The bombs dropped were devastating — lighting the area up in fire and smoke.

We resided in a two-segment apartment building. Our apartment was in the feeble, two-storey segment situated in front of the better-constructed six-storey portion. Two bombs — one containing conventional heavy explosives followed by an incendiary bomb — landed right on top of the six-storey part of our building. Several people were killed instantly. As fire rapidly spread, we were all in a severe state of shock except for my father, who had been a medic in World War I and knew how to remain calm. He told us that panicking was the worst thing we could do and that if we kept our cool we would all be okay. He added that we didn't have much time, so we all had to listen carefully to his instructions.

The plan, he said, was for all of us to meet at Uncle Chaim's place. My uncle lived with his family at 48 Pawia Street, several blocks away from us. Looking out the window, my dad had quickly surveyed the damage in the area and figured Uncle Chaim's building was in a part of the neighbourhood that had not been hit. If he was wrong about that, our orders were to go to Uncle Jankiel's, who lived even further away from us.

My dad told my sister, Brenda, to grab my hand and for the two of us to leave first. He said we were not to separate under any circumstances. As Brenda and I scrambled out the door, I heard my father yell out, "God be with you!"

Out in the streets, tenants of several bombed high-rises in the area were running around in a state of panic. We ran carefully from house to house, dodging the Luftwaffe's bombs.

Our neighbourhood was engulfed in flames, the blaze coming from many buildings. And once the fire had burned all it could, what was left of the buildings came crashing to the ground. Meanwhile, the German planes kept coming. Whenever one squadron would fly off and it looked like it was all over, another would come in and continue to pound us.

We kept running and tried to block out all the chaos. My sister stayed in control by repeatedly saying, "God is with us. We will make it, Jankiel, we will make it." I couldn't stop thinking about what was happening to my parents. If they were dead, I asked myself, what would happen to us?

It took about an hour and a half, but we were lucky enough to make it to my uncle's place. My sister and I embraced when we entered the apartment building. The bombing had quieted down, and it seemed that my uncle's area of the Jewish quarter had not been hit.

Tears of joy and sorrow trickled down my cheeks. I was elated that we had survived, but gravely concerned that no one else from our family had arrived yet. But Brenda held firmly to her faith that all would be well. "Don't cry, Jankiel. You'll see, they will soon be here," she said while hugging me tightly. "Just wait and see, they'll be here soon." We passed the time by describing to Uncle Chaim and Auntie Sarah how our place had been burned to the ground and that much of our street was ablaze.

The rest of my family arrived about thirty minutes later. We all hugged each other and thanked God for guiding us safely to the apartment.

The ecstasy of seeing everyone again, however, soon wore off. They hadn't brought anything with them — not even the seven loaves of bread for which we had stood in line for hours. All we had were the clothes on our backs. Fortunately, Uncle Chaim and Auntie Sarah had some food they were willing to share with us.

Like my father, my uncle was a tradesman who made fur collars for the clothing trade. He had twelve children — six boys and six girls. I vividly remember how my mother used to prepare and deliver food parcels for them. While our family incomes were comparable, my parents were better off because they had only five children at home. I know we could have used the extra food, but my mother was an extremely good-hearted and charitable woman. I remember she used to say to us that God would reward us for taking care of others in need.

"If we're capable, we have to help them," she would say. "If we give, we will also receive in turn."

But now we were all struggling to get by. Because of the bombing, we had lost everything. That included my father's equipment, and operating those machines was all he knew. We had no idea what he would now do for a living without them. We would soon also learn that my mother's mother lost both her orchard and her farm when they were expropriated by the Nazis.

For the moment, though, we had our immediate concerns — trying to survive as we stayed with Uncle Chaim. Their place was small and crowded; fourteen of them already lived uncomfortably by having to share only two rooms — one of which was a kitchen. With seven more people, there were now twenty-one bodies crammed into the apartment. Things would have been even worse if more relatives had turned up. My father had five brothers and five sisters, and all had children of their own.

My dad realized how difficult it would be to stay with so many people in such a small place, and so the following morning he told us we would try to make it to Uncle Jankiel's. He and his wife, Hanna, were my favourites. They were the most affluent of all my aunts and uncles and would bring some kind of treat whenever they visited us. Like my father, Uncle Jankiel made shoes, but he had a larger operation. He also had only three children to take care of, a small family at that time. They lived in a four-room apartment, which included a cellar used as a workshop for making shoes. We hoped they would let us stay in the cellar.

We were physically and emotionally exhausted from the ordeal of the day, so we had no problem falling asleep that night as we crammed together on Uncle Chaim's apartment floor. The bombing started again the next day, causing us to postpone our move to Uncle Jankiel's by twenty-four hours. When the bombing subsided somewhat on the third day, we bade tearful farewells to Uncle Chaim and his family and made it over to Uncle Jankiel's, where he promptly took us to the basement. His own family had already moved down there. Under the constant threat of bombing, they were safer in the basement than in their above-ground apartment. As we expected, Uncle Jankiel was generous. He and his family shared all their food with us and sacrificed their furniture as firewood for cooking and heat.

The next day, my oldest brother, Getzel, ventured back to our old home to survey the damage and to see if he could collect anything. He found the place had been totally obliterated; only the foundation remained. He returned with tears in his eyes. "It's all gone, Mom," he said as he hugged my mother. "Everything's gone. But at least we are all alive and that means everything," he added as they started to cry. It was so strange to see Getzel, who had always been so happy, cry.

We all had tears in our eyes as we realized that all our possessions and any remnants of our past had been destroyed. My mother was extremely distressed — not even a single photograph had been saved. As my sister hugged my mother, she offered a typical dose of optimism through her own tears: "When peace sets in, we will make it back again," she said. "We will build it all up again. We can get new furniture and clothing."

～

Warsaw was under siege for the rest of the month. The German attack was particularly vicious on September 13, which was the eve of Rosh Hashanah — the Jewish New Year. Artillery fire accompanied heavy aerial bombardments, and Warsaw lay in ruins. Yet the Germans continued to bomb the city. Toward the end of September, they intensified their efforts.

There was no gas, heat or hydro that month. Just getting adequate food and water was no easy task. For water, residents had to reach the Vistula River or crowd around bomb craters filled with rain. A major advantage to our location was that we were only two blocks from the Vistula, so water was not a major issue.

As for food, we shared all of my uncle's, but that didn't last long. Most stores had been destroyed in the bombings, and all the food had disappeared from the shelves earlier in the month anyway. To eat, we had to get creative. People killed their pets for meat, and others looked for stray animals in the streets.

One day, Getzel heard that a pickling plant was on fire, and despite the dangers of the streets he waded through the war zone to get to the facility. He returned with two large containers of pickles. Getzel risked his life for the meal, but soon after eating all the pickles, we realized fasting that night would have been better than ingesting those things. They were spoiled rotten, and we all ended up with severe stomach cramps.

Another time, we heard there was a ship in the harbour that had caught fire. Its cargo was said to contain rice. Getzel risked his life again to trek to the ship, where he filled a large pillowcase with rice before returning safely. Many others died trying to get this rice, engulfed by the fire or killed by falling debris.

That rice became our main source of food for several days. We cooked it over an open fire, breaking furniture into small pieces to use as precious firewood.

One of the best meals we had came after a Polish army horse was killed by shrapnel on the street in front of our building. My father was one of many men who rushed out to carve a piece of the dead animal. He brought back a large chunk, and with the rice we had what felt like a feast.

For the short term we survived, but we knew we couldn't live this way forever. And we figured it wouldn't be long before Warsaw fell to the Germans and Poland would capitulate. Everyone knew that the Polish army, which still had only a cavalry of horses in many places, was no match for the mechanized strength of the German army. Poland had no choice but to give up unconditionally. On September 27, the country surrendered.

Warsaw was a disaster area. Fires were still raging, buildings had been flattened, and people were in a state of shock and disbelief. September had been a month of nothing but death and destruction.

We knew the Germans would arrive in a few days and expected them to rebuild Warsaw — the city would survive. But as Jews, we were worried about our future. We had heard what the Germans had done to Jews in their country — the harassment, the vandalism, the violence. Even so, we had no idea how bad it would get.

The German army, with all its might of tanks and trucks, rolled into Warsaw on September 29, 1939. I vividly remember how the tall men in their fancy uniforms and high leather boots marched in as if they were great heroes. It was a large, colourful parade, complete with loud bands playing. The Nazis projected an image of invincibility — that they would take over the world and have little difficulty in doing it.

Days after taking control, the Germans began their program of tyranny against the Jews, and they had support in their efforts from many Poles who were antisemitic. With the city in shambles, the conquerors established bread lines to feed the masses. Poles and Jews were fed separately, with the Jews getting far less. Many Jews joined Polish lines. Some Poles who didn't know any German quickly learned how to say "Ein Jude" (a Jew) to identify the Jews in the line. Often to a chorus of laughter, young German soldiers would pull the Jews aside and beat them senseless.

The Nazis also confiscated Jewish property and enacted a series of increasingly harsh anti-Jewish decrees. To start, Jews had to turn over all their gold, silver and jewellery. There were serious repercussions for anyone caught withholding their valuables. Jews were also rounded up for forced labour and treated brutally in the process. The Nazis would take women, for instance, and force them to clean toilets using their underwear as wash rags. Meanwhile, elderly Orthodox men who just happened to be walking down the street would have their beards chopped off before being savagely beaten.

On top of this, many Poles would perpetrate violent acts against Jews, much to the pleasure of the Germans. This terror was made more convenient in November when the Germans decreed that all Jews older than ten were to wear white armbands displaying a blue Star of David. Facing such a frightening climate of hostility, most Jews were scared to even leave their apartments.

~

We knew we were an unfair burden on Uncle Jankiel, so my parents and my siblings and I left his home soon after the Germans arrived. Because we couldn't afford rent anywhere, we went back to our old building, which was now just a burned-out shell of a structure. With nothing remaining of our apartment, we made our way down to the building's cellar. There was a small room down there, which became our home until we could accumulate some money. There was no heating and no floor — just black soil. We laid some boards down and covered them with blankets Uncle Jankiel had given us. Staying there was incredibly dangerous, since the whole building could have collapsed on top of us at any time. But it was the only free accommodation we could think of.

My mother managed to scrounge up some money and belongings from her relatives to get us started on the road to recovery. She sold these items in the street markets, which were the main form of commerce in the Jewish area. The shops never recovered from all the damage they had sustained, and prices had become so expensive that haggling on the street was the only practical way the community could function. By the end of November, the sidewalks were filled with people bartering for the necessities of life.

Eventually, my mother made enough złotys from shrewd buying and selling to get us into a little place in the Jewish neighbourhood at 64 Miła Street. It had one large room with a kitchen. My sister slept in the kitchen, while the rest of us shared the other room.

My father became seriously ill before the end of the year with a kidney disease. We could not afford any medicine — not that there was any available — but he managed to slowly recover. Even when he felt well physically, he struggled mentally and emotionally because he couldn't work at his trade. He had no equipment, and with the extreme poverty that had set in, he had few potential customers. In time, his depression led to renewed deterioration of his physical condition, and he became increasingly weak and vulnerable.

With my father unable to cope, my oldest brother Getzel had to take on more responsibility for supporting the family. Getzel had always been my idol. He had been an excellent soccer goalie, and I had loved to watch him play. He was also a great dancer and popular with girls. Before the war, he had been a fun-loving young man. Despite our upbringing, he had no interest in religion, though he used to go through the motions and say prayers with us each day to please my mother.

Now he was doing what he could to support our family — until one day in early 1940 when he was plucked off the street by the Germans, pushed into a truck and forced to remove snow from the streets. At the end of the day, some of these workers were sent to labour camps. Getzel was among the fortunate who were sent home, but the experience had a profound impact on him.

His first words to us that evening were, "Mom and Dad, I'm leaving tomorrow for the Soviet Union." He said lots of people were doing it every day. Before Germany declared war on the Soviet Union, it was easier for people to find ways to cross the border.

He explained to my parents that he was going with his friend Herschel. Herschel was not just any friend — he was Brenda's boyfriend. He and my sister were even talking about marriage at the time.

Both Getzel and Herschel wanted to take Brenda with them, pleading with my mother that they would take good care of her. My sister desperately wanted to go with them, but my mother wouldn't allow it. She said Getzel and Herschel were slightly older than Brenda and they were men, so they'd be able to handle the rough journey. She insisted it would be too difficult for Brenda. My mom also argued it was bad enough that she had to lose her first-born; she said two children leaving the family was too much. However, she did offer a compromise to keep Brenda happy. Getzel and Herschel were to report back on their status, and when my mom was satisfied that all was well for them in the Soviet Union, our family would make every effort to move east to join them.

Early the next day, Getzel threw a few things in a handbag, and my mother gave him whatever money she could spare. There were lots of hugs, kisses and tears as he left.

About a week passed before we received a letter from Białystok, a Polish city on the border with the Soviet Union. Getzel wrote that he had applied for a work visa at the Soviet consulate in Białystok. He made it clear that he didn't care where he would live in the Soviet Union; he just wanted to stay away from Poland. He also mentioned that my mother was wise not to send Brenda because the waiting compound was disgusting. Lice were everywhere, there were no facilities to bathe or do laundry, and people had to sleep on a floor of dirt.

The next letter we received came from Getzel in the Soviet Union. He had finally acquired a Soviet visa. Like most people who fled Poland, he had been sent to the Ural Mountains, an area just west of Siberia, and was assigned work as a bricklayer. He wrote regularly from his address at Berezniki, Molotovskaya Oblast (now Permskaya Oblast), an address that has been firmly planted in my memory since the first time I saw it on an envelope.

Judging by his letters, he was doing fine. He wrote that he was treated well at his job and enjoyed studying Russian in the evenings. He enclosed photos of himself on construction sites with some of his new Russian friends dressed in their big puffy jackets as they braved the −40° c cold.

As for Herschel, he had received approval to enter the Soviet Union a week or two after Getzel. However, instead of going to Siberia as instructed, he told the Soviets he'd rather stay near the border so he'd be relatively close to Brenda. This did not please the authorities. Like many others who voiced their preferences, Herschel was considered a traitor, and as punishment was sent to a forced labour camp. Although that may seem cruel, it was much better than being sent back to Poland. Returning into the hands of the Nazis would have meant certain death. At least in the forced labour camps there was a good chance of survival. At the end of the war, many of the prisoners were able to come back to Poland to search for survivors, though I don't know what happened to Herschel after being sent away.

Getzel applied for papers to bring all of us to the Soviet Union, but he warned that it would take time to work through the bureaucracy. I remember my mother crying the day she received that letter from Getzel. She cried partly for joy, that one day we'd be able to move, and partly out of sorrow at the thought of abandoning her mother, who at eighty was too old to be accepted by the Soviets. She also worried about all her relatives and all the other Jews in Poland who would have to live under Nazi occupation.

Unfortunately, we never had the chance to leave anyone behind.

In June 1941, Germany invaded the Soviet Union. We lost contact with my brother and never heard from him again. I do not know what happened to him. Maybe he was conscripted into the army and killed in battle. Whatever his fate, I hope it was better than what was to come for the rest of us in Poland.

Piercing the Walls

In the early winter months of 1940, before the Germans invaded the Soviet Union and we were still receiving letters from my brother, life was becoming increasingly difficult for us under German rule. Without Getzel to help us, I began working the streets to try to get food for my family. Using skills I had learned from watching my mother, I took several small items from our apartment and sold them on the city's street markets. With that money, I bought cigarettes, which I offered to farmers who had set up stalls in the markets. I knew that most of these men were smokers but unable to leave their stalls to buy cigarettes, so they would pay me extra to deliver them.

I would get up very early in the morning before the sunrise when my mom would make a breakfast of potato soup for me. Then I was off. Because we didn't have enough money for leather, I wore wooden shoes, which gave no protection from the −20° C temperature. Most people got by with bare feet, even in the snow. I was one of the lucky ones who had wooden shoes. I just had to do my best to block out the cold as I went to the corner of Lubeckiego and Miła streets, where I bought a load of Junaki cigarettes, the cheapest brand available. By about halfway through the morning, I had usually sold about two hundred of them. That earned me enough of a profit to purchase a one-kilogram loaf of rye bread and a couple of potatoes. I was proud of myself each day I brought that food home, and I knew my parents were proud of me too.

Our family needed more than just my efforts to feed us. My older brother Menashe also sold cigarettes, operating a few blocks away from me so we wouldn't compete with one another. My mother and sister also helped out by selling small items at the bazaar on Smocza Street.

We probably wouldn't have survived had we not gathered all that extra food on our own. Rations were supplied to the Jews, but it wasn't enough food to survive on, and even by early 1940 the suffering resulting from malnutrition had become apparent. The situation worsened at an accelerated pace. The Germans wanted Jews from in and around Warsaw concentrated in the city's Jewish quarter. The population density in that small area increased daily.

In the second half of 1940, German plans for the Warsaw ghetto came into focus. In August, they announced that there were to be three zones — German, Polish and Jewish — with the Jews not allowed to enter into the German area. In October, it was announced that the Jews were to be contained by brick walls.

By the end of November 1940, construction of the enclosure was complete. The ghetto walls were about ten feet high, up to twenty feet in spots, and topped with crushed glass. There were German and Polish guards at all the entrances, and only those few Jews with the appropriate work permits were permitted to leave, while Poles were forbidden from entering. The ghetto area of 3.4 square kilometres was completely cut off from the rest of the city.

Meanwhile, as less and less food was made available, disease began to also take its toll. With the Germans progressively reducing the water supply, proper sanitation was an impossibility and lice became ubiquitous. Outbreaks of typhus, tuberculosis and diphtheria became major problems. It was just what the Germans wanted, giving them the opportunity to post signs designating the Jewish area as a "plague-infested" zone to be avoided.

Under such duress, many who didn't die of starvation or disease saw only a grim future for themselves and withered away with broken hearts. It felt as though there wasn't even fresh air because there were hardly any trees; the boundaries of the ghetto excluded all parks and playgrounds. It was just one big mass of human misery and suffering.

For my family and me, life also went from bad to worse. Before the walls were erected, we were able to effectively acquire food, but the walls isolated us from our food source. Officially, the rule in January 1941 was that any adult Jew caught on the "Aryan" side outside the ghetto received a 1,000 złoty fine and three months in jail. Toward the end of the year, the penalty changed to the death sentence. Although the law was more lenient for children, the reality was that the wall was patrolled by men with guns who were free to shoot or severely beat anyone who tried to cross — whatever their age.

Closed off from the outside world, most children took to the ghetto streets to beg for food. But there were thousands of children and precious little food. I realized this tactic was sure to lead to starvation and saw only one solution; somehow, I had to leave the ghetto to get food.

My first foray outside the ghetto involved a friend of mine named Sewek, a brash boy about four years older than me. He lived in our building, and our families knew each other well. Sewek and I agreed to establish a business partnership smuggling food into the ghetto. I'm certain we were among the first Warsaw ghetto smugglers.

Sewek had some money, which we used to get ourselves started. We found a hole in the wall and slipped into the "Aryan" section. We used his money to buy food — bread, marmalade, sausage and other essentials. We took it all back wrapped in bedspreads and pillowcases, which meant our return to the ghetto was even riskier than our exit. Fortunately, we weren't caught.

After providing our parents with enough food for our families, we then offered the rest to other Jews in the ghetto in exchange for valuables such as watches or jewellery. We took those items back over to the "Aryan" side and sold them for a good sum of money, which we used to get more food. This cycle went on for a couple of trips. We ended the day with a significant profit.

I had thought Sewek and I agreed to be equal partners, but after that successful first day of working together, he kept 75 per cent for himself and refused to consider giving me more. As a result, I broke off our partnership and the next day tried to operate alone. To get myself started, I asked my sister if she could part with her one and only fancy dress. I knew it could sell for enough money to kick-start my scheme. She wasn't happy to do so, but in a typical display of kindness she gave it to me and wished me luck.

Within a few trips, I had my family fed and could start thinking of making a small profit. I was particularly proud that I was doing better than Sewek. By the time I completed two or three trips, he was just finishing his first.

More children started to smuggle, although we were never more than a select minority. We were resourceful, using whatever means was available to get out of the ghetto. We were small, which meant we were often able to get through small drainage holes in the bottom of the walls or other holes that adults made for us. We also broke through ourselves by chipping away one brick at a time until there was a hole big enough to just squeeze through. Often, the German guards and Polish police would find our holes and fill them in, so we would always be looking to punch out new ones to stay one step ahead of them.

When it wasn't possible to go through the wall, we went over it. This was the more difficult way because we had to scale all the brick and then manoeuvre across the crushed glass cemented at the top. We put thick rags over the glass so we could stay at the top for a few moments before jumping down. Even after getting to the other side, we were only partway to safety. With guards buzzing around the wall and all its entrances, there was no assurance we'd get away from the wall undetected.

This dangerous, hustling lifestyle quickly came to dominate my childhood. It was depressing to realize that other children were playing with toys while I was risking my life to feed my family. My only breaks came on the weekends. I would not smuggle on Saturdays, the Jewish Sabbath, or Sundays when all the stores were closed on the "Aryan" side.

Just as he did before the walls were erected, my older brother Menashe did his best to smuggle too. Unfortunately, he was never comfortable with the task. He had a quiet, passive personality — similar to my father. He loved to sing and paint. If the war had not destroyed our lives, I think my parents would have tried to save their money to send him to Paris to go to art school. I don't think he ever would have been much of a businessman. My mother and sister were busy taking care of my father. He was getting weaker by the day.

Sometimes when I smuggled, it was too risky to return, and I had to stay on the "Aryan" side overnight. That made for a dangerous situation, but I was fortunate I became friends with a Polish couple who helped me. Mr. and Mrs. Slawcia were a middle-aged couple who did not have any children of their own. They knew I was Jewish but always supported me. They let me stay with them when I couldn't get back to the ghetto — which was especially important on the bitterly cold days of winter.

The couple owned a cafe on Grochowska Street in the Praga district of Warsaw. Their cafe was small — only four tables — but it was always full, so they managed to earn a decent living. I would often bring them small items from my bartering, and in return they fed me their specialty — sausage and sauerkraut. They also distilled whisky in their home. When I would drink it, my tongue would go numb from its potency. But I didn't let that deter me. I felt I was enduring the hardships of an adult, so I was entitled to behave — and drink — like one.

Most of my excursions to the "Aryan" side went well, though I was caught several times. On a few occasions, the police gave me painful beatings with their hard rubber sticks. When they caught me, they would confiscate all the goods I had accumulated. To protect myself from being put in jail, I used my little brother Eli's identity papers to show that I was only eight years old, which is about how old I looked. They'd see those papers and release me to my sister with a warning not to do it again.

The documents helped but they guaranteed nothing. One day a Polish police officer caught me on the "Aryan" side and took me to a jail. They didn't even bother to look at my papers. Fortunately, it was assumed that I was just a Polish youth who was stealing some small goods. Not long before that I had bought a cross, which I wore around my neck to protect my identity.

I was also helped by not having a typically Jewish appearance. I had a small nose, kept my hair short and spoke fluent Polish. So it was natural for them to assume I was Polish, and I wasn't going to argue. I just told them that I was an eight-year-old from outside Warsaw and that I was deeply sorry for being a troublemaker.

While processing the paperwork for my release, they put me in a room with a twelve-year-old boy. The security was not particularly tight as our second-floor cell had a regular glass window without any bars. The boy I was with said he had been caught before, so he expected to soon be taken away to a more secure jail. He decided that if he was ever going to escape, he would have to do it from our holding cell. He smashed the window and jumped to the ground. That was as far as he got. I think he broke both his legs when he hit the ground, and the authorities did not look pleased when they took him away, possibly to be shot. Soon after he jumped, I was released. I knew if I was caught a second time they would not be as lenient with me, and they reminded me of that on my way out.

The scariest moment I ever had crossing the wall came at the hands of a vicious German we called Frankenstein.[1] In 1941, he was assigned patrol duty of the Stawki Street wall, with his home station at the gate on the corner of Żelazna and Leszno streets.

Frankenstein was a short, bull-legged, creepy-looking man. He loved to hunt, but I suppose he must have become bored with animals and decided that shooting Jewish children was a more enjoyable pastime. The younger the children, the more he enjoyed shooting them. He killed and injured so many that it became necessary to open a surgical emergency clinic in my former school, which was in his patrolling vicinity.

He guarded the area in a jeep with a mounted machine gun. As children climbed the wall, Frankenstein and a German assistant would zoom in from out of nowhere on their killing machine. The other guy always drove so Frankenstein had quick access to his machine gun.

Once he spotted someone, there was no time for them to hide — it didn't matter whether they were in the process of climbing or just near the wall and getting ready. It took only seconds from the time he eyed someone until the moment he murdered them with a spray of bullets.

When there were no climbers to kill, he would summon ghetto kids who happened to be in his line of sight — a long way from the wall and with no intention of going anywhere. Typically, he would just yell out "Jude" (Jew), and that was it — their life was over. When he called, kids had to walk toward him, and he would yell at them

---

1   Josef Blösche was a Nazi guard notorious for his cruelty toward Jews in the Warsaw ghetto. Over two decades after the war, he was tried and executed for war crimes.

for a moment and then say they were free to leave. Moments later, he would pull out his pistol and shoot them in the back of the head. After his successful hunt, he'd walk to his jeep and drive off until the next time — and no one knew when or where that would be.

All of us smugglers were terrified of him. But we had no choice. We had to eat.

One day as I entered the ghetto over the Stawki wall with a bag full of food I was bringing back from the gentile market, I stood still, scouting around before I left the wall. Frankenstein drove quickly toward the wall, shooting his gun to get my attention.

He pulled up in front of me and yelled for me to walk toward him. A numb feeling gripped my body. I knew right then and there that my life was over. He was going to kill me, probably with a bullet to my head.

I wanted it to be over as quickly as possible. I hated his guts and visualized myself spitting in his face before he killed me. Fortunately, I restrained myself from doing that. I wouldn't be here to write this story if I had.

Propelled by the adrenaline rush of impending death, words started pouring out of my mouth in a desperate attempt to save my skin. I was actually trying to convince the cold-blooded monster that he was making a mistake. "I don't understand what you are saying," I pleaded. "I am a Catholic boy," I cried, supported by the fact that I had a cross around my neck.

"I'm just trying to make a few złotys for my poor parents. Father is sick with a heart condition. I need to make a little money to put some food on our table." My whole spiel was in Polish, and the German Frankenstein couldn't understand a word of it. I kept rambling at him as he carried on a discussion with his assistant.

I had the feeling Frankenstein's partner was a *Volksdeutscher*, a Pole with German heritage who was from somewhere near the German border. He seemed to understand my Polish. He looked at me intently when I spoke and was fixated on the cross I wore around my neck.

It was a pathetic scene, but the pleading was my only chance. Showing off the cross hanging from my neck, I started to recite all the Catholic prayers I knew. I figured that if I could plant a seed of doubt in their minds, they might think I really was a gentile. I begged incessantly, crying out for them to believe me. I promised that I would never again come to the ghetto and deal with the Jews. With a bag full of smuggled goods in hand, I could tell I hadn't fully convinced them, but thanks to the cross, the assistant wasn't entirely convinced I was Jewish either.

That *Volksdeutscher* lobbied on my behalf, but my fate was still in Frankenstein's hands. They talked it over for a few moments — the Polish man doing most of the talking, gesturing with his hands. Frankenstein was tapping his fully drawn gun in his palm, probably salivating about the prospect of blowing my brains out.

When they stopped talking, they came closer to me. Frankenstein just stood there staring down at me — mumbling something that I couldn't understand. A moment later, he motioned for me to walk away.

I figured that the next event was a bullet in the back of my head. That made me even more desperate. To his surprise, I raced toward him, grabbed his pant leg and knelt down on one knee. Pretending to be a Catholic preparing for death, I used my hand and traced a cross on my chest.

He was unfazed. He still had his gun in hand ready to shoot me. I got up to take the final few paces of my life but slowly walked away from him backwards, so we continued to face one another. If he was going to kill me, he would have to do it on my terms, not in his cowardly way. Shockingly, he didn't shoot. Instead, he ran over and gave me a kick in the butt with his huge, heavy boots. He packed his gun away and yelled at me to get lost. They got in the jeep and drove off; he really was letting me go.

I was incredibly lucky. I think if that *Volksdeutscher* hadn't been Frankenstein's partner, I would not have survived. As happened so many times in the war, I may have been in the wrong place, but I was lucky to be caught there at the right time.

The instantaneous high of dodging death momentarily drowned out the agonizing pain of Frankenstein's forceful kick as I ran to a nearby building. A group of people had gathered in a second-storey window to watch the incident unfold. Crying with joy, they came down to see me and started kissing me.

"We expected to be burying you, not talking to you," one of them said, not believing what she had just seen. "He let you go with just a kick in the ass? What did you say to him that he let you live? Tell us, tell us. No one has ever escaped him before."

Said another: "My boy, you have just been reborn. You escaped the devil himself. If he did not take your life, it means God is good to you. He wants you to live. You are going to survive the war. Yes, you will survive the war. If you can make it past him, you can make it past anyone."

I couldn't believe what had happened. I literally pinched myself to make sure it was real. It's still hard to believe I survived. For a few days after the event, word got around about what had happened. It seemed everyone in the ghetto knew about it.

I was thrilled at my good fortune but at the same time the whole incident left me traumatized. I felt like a walking ghost, knowing that I really should have been dead. Emotionally, I never fully recovered from that incident, and it took several days and several nightmares before I even became functional again. On top of that, he had kicked me so hard I could barely walk for days.

Even after the terror of Frankenstein, I had no choice but to go back to smuggling even though I hated doing it. I blocked out the fear as best I could and day after day forced myself to go. Hunger forces people to take risks. How was my family going to eat if I didn't smuggle?

I did have moments when I nearly gave up.

Once, I was caught right outside the ghetto and taken to the Gestapo headquarters to be interrogated. They weren't fooling around, and I was sure I was dead. Just the way they stared at me made sweat pour down my forehead.

With the cross around my neck, I again pretended I was a gentile child. But I was also prepared to give in if it came to that. The anguish was beginning to be too much, and I thought life could mercifully end if I gave up. However, I can honestly say I heard little voices in my head telling me not to surrender — to stick to my story.

As two men came over to interrogate me, I kissed my cross and said a prayer loudly in Polish. One of them spoke Polish and again interpreted for the other. I told them I was only smuggling to support my poor Polish family and that I would never do it again. I begged them to release me because my family would be getting worried if I didn't return soon. After thirty minutes, they told me I'd be released as long as I promised never to go near the ghetto again, and they told me to tell my father to get a job so I wouldn't have to put myself at risk again.

I thanked them, promised I wouldn't do it again, and ran off. Once again, I couldn't believe my good fortune to be in the clutches of the Germans and escape. As I walked away, I kept thinking of the little voices I heard telling me not to give up. I inhaled a few breaths of delicious fresh air and dashed home.

I often had more guts than brains during those smuggling days. I also had a lot of luck. When I got caught a couple more times after that incident, I fed them my standard story of being a gentile boy trying to earn a few bucks selling food to the Jews. Each time, they just told me to go home and never come near the ghetto again. I thanked them in Polish, crossed my heart, and left by saying: "Thank you, Jesus, for guiding me."

Since I was fortunate to be caught by different men on each of those occasions, I got away with little more than a scolding. Perhaps the jails became overcrowded, or it was my appearance, or maybe it was because I was handled by soft, lazy or stupid people, but whatever the reason, I managed to slip through the cracks of the system. Somehow they believed my story — they didn't take me to the Gestapo headquarters where all they had to do to check my identity was take my pants down to reveal my circumcised penis.

~

The smuggling and hand-to-mouth existence I had to endure for so long gave me a cynical view of the world during the crucial, formative years of childhood. Yet no matter how bad conditions became, my family and I never lost hope. We thought one day the Germans would be defeated and life would return to normal. Until then, our approach was to live for the moment, hoping to still be around the next hour and the next day, and hoping that soon life would get better. We had to believe that. Survival is impossible without hope, even if the hope is false hope.

Devastation at Home

The contrast between the ghetto and the outside world was chilling. The "Aryan" side seemed like heaven. People were working and food was available. Conditions were more difficult than usual, but there still was a sense of normalcy.

Inside the ghetto, there was nothing but misery. By early 1941, malnutrition was replaced by mass starvation. It became common to see men, women and especially children dying in the streets. Corpses were dragged off the sidewalks for mass burials of fifty at a time. When someone died, others stole the clothes off the dead body. The corpse was then covered with newspapers until the collecting wagons came along. Eventually, people became so accustomed to death that no one even bothered to cover the bodies anymore.

Each time I returned to the ghetto, my first sight was countless tiny, starving children begging for scraps of food. Many didn't even look human anymore. They were on death's doorstep, either so seriously malnourished their bellies distended like giant balloons or so thin they were nothing more than skin-and-bone. I always tore one of my loaves of bread into small bits and placed them in the skinny little hands of some of these children. It was heart-wrenching to see such a pathetic sight. Each day, I arrived home with tears in my eyes.

With scores of people dying daily under the inhuman conditions of the ghetto, it was only a matter of time before someone in my family would succumb. Already in a weakened physical and mental state, my father was the first to die. Not long after becoming seriously ill — about seven months after the ghetto was established — he died battling a mysterious disease my mother refused to talk about. All I remember is that the problem involved his kidneys.

My father stood about six feet, two inches tall, weighed around two hundred pounds and was a handsome man with lots of curly hair. At least that's the image I remember of him — not what he looked like when he died, which bore no resemblance to his appearance from before the war.

As we became poorer and poorer, my father started to become more and more depressed. All he knew was how to make fur accessories and sandals. He had no other means to support the family. He had to watch me take to the streets early each morning while he sat idly by, as though I were the father and he the child. For a man who had always worked hard to sustain his family, it was a dreadful thing to have to go through. This helplessness fuelled his poor health. He was so ill he always slept on the only bed in our cramped apartment.

My father's plight was typical of what happened to many adults in the ghetto. The only ones who had any chance to survive were the street-savvy, rough, tough, dealmakers. My activities brought me into contact with these big-time smugglers. They would bribe guards to bring wagons of stuff into the ghetto. Although they had a certain callousness to ignore all the misery of fellow Jews, I admired these gangster-like figures. They were just doing what was necessary to survive. I became friends with some of them, and they often used me as an errand boy.

There was such a stark contrast between those smugglers and my father. My dad was just a kind-hearted, simple, family man. He was doomed in the ghetto. I could see his condition deteriorating more each day. He lost about sixty pounds in a matter of weeks, and even though a large portion of my smuggling earnings went toward medicine for him, it was to no avail. A doctor visited frequently and would tell us he could not prevent the inevitable.

My father died one night in the spring of 1941. He was forty-four years old. By the time he passed away, thousands of people had lost their lives in the ghetto, but none had been from my immediate family. I had just turned ten and was devastated.

The next day was a cool, cloudy Friday — another depressing day in the ghetto. People came with a wagon to take my father's body away, as though he were a piece of trash. Men from our building — including my friend Sewek — acted as pseudo-pallbearers, carrying his corpse to the wagon.

He was just piled on. The wagon was filled with bodies, and on its way to collect a few more before going to the Jewish cemetery for yet another day of mass burials. The whole process lacked even a shred of decency.

After my dad's body was picked up, my family went to the cemetery. We arrived at about midday, and within a few minutes Menashe spotted my father's remains from among about fifty bodies lying on a large table. After waiting around for two long hours until the rabbi arrived, my father and the other dead men and boys were wrapped in a large tallis (a prayer shawl) and thrown into a mass grave. The rabbi, an old man with a long white beard, told us to say Kaddish, the Jewish prayer for the dead. Word for word, my brothers and I recited the prayer — hopeful that my dad's soul would reach heaven and be embraced by God. My father deserved to go to heaven. He was a sincere, honest, hard-working man. Unfortunately, he was taken away from me in what should have been the prime of his life.

At the funeral, my mother tried hard to hold her tears back. The rest of us cried openly, as any children would at a parent's funeral. However, given the circumstances of the ghetto, this funeral was much more sombre than those of normal times. I was traumatized for months; night after night, I dreamed about all those bodies lying on that table.

The only morsel of satisfaction was that we were able to see my dad laid to rest at least partially in accordance with Jewish tradition. I was also somewhat comforted by the rabbi when he told me it was only my father's body that had died — that his soul was on its way to heaven. As I kept telling my mother, at least we had the rest of the family for support.

When the ceremony ended, there was nowhere to go but home, and there wasn't anything good to go home to. In some ways, my dad was better off. At least his troubles were over; ours were just beginning.

It wasn't long after my father died that my mother began to take a major turn for the worse herself. It was extremely painful to watch her deteriorate each day. I had always been close to my mother and have many fond memories of her. Her final days are not among them.

The good days were when I was about seven years old, and I would work with her during my summer holidays. After helping her set up a booth to sell sandals at the farmers' market, it was my job to protect the merchandise so she could concentrate on sales. Thieves were all over the place, and we had to be vigilant to avoid being victimized. There was no end to the threats.

Those days at the market gave me a chance to watch my mother in action. I had great respect for her talents. Working with her offered a great education in the fundamentals of business and how to properly treat customers. I would not have survived on the streets of Warsaw had it not been for what she taught me.

Her business acumen led to one of my most successful smuggling ventures. In late 1941, when the Germans were in desperate need of warm clothes for the Soviet front, a decree was issued that forbade Jewish women from possessing any fur. Even if all they had was a fur collar, Jews were forced to hand all their fur pieces over to the Germans during door-to-door collections.

Many Jewish women owned furs and would do anything they could to avoid giving theirs to the Germans. People would bury their fur items deep in the ground in boxes, hoping to retrieve them when the war ended. Unfortunately, fur dries out and goes rotten when stored this way, leaving the coat worthless — though even the people who knew this felt burying the garment was much better than giving it to the Germans.

Late in the summer of 1941, well before the Germans issued their decree but at a time when everyone knew it would happen sooner or later, my mother suggested that I buy furs cheaply from Jews before they had to turn them over. I would then sneak out to sell them to women outside the ghetto for a decent profit.

After I succeeded with this and other smuggling schemes, my mother would say how proud she was of me. She told me that I had a good head for business and that one day I would grow up to be a successful businessman. That gave me a valuable boost of confidence.

"I will be so proud of you when you grow up and do well for yourself," she would say. "Not that I am not proud of you now. I am. I'm proud of all of you. You are wonderful children who any mother would be happy to have. I look forward to the day when you're all grown up and have children of your own."

My mother was a tough woman, but above all she was a dedicated mother who adored her children. She would — and did — give her life for her kids.

My mother had been such a vibrant and beautiful woman, which made it unbearable to see what she had become in the ghetto. Like my father, she was broken-hearted, feeling totally helpless as she watched her children suffer. It seemed she had lost the will to live. She was starving herself to death — insisting that her meagre bread ration go to Eli, as well as her portion of whatever food I smuggled home. As death approached, I suppose the only thing she could look forward to was spending eternity with my father, whom she missed dearly.

In the end, her mental and emotional depression led to physical illness in the form of a liver problem, and she went to her grave only months after my father's death. I had lost both my parents by September 1941.

What made it even more difficult for me was that I was not with my mom when she succumbed. I was out hustling on the "Aryan" side all day, and when I returned in the evening I heard crying as soon as I walked through the door. I knew right away that she had died. I burst out crying. I loved her so much — and still miss her greatly.

Like my father, she was tossed onto a cart along with several other bodies that had been collected off the streets. This time, however, we never even got to see her remains because she was immediately buried in a mass grave. The undertakers were digging countless graves per day by then and dumping wagons full of bodies into them like garbage. All we could do was say Kaddish with the man responsible for the burials.

With both my parents gone, Brenda took over the reins of the household. She was a lovely young woman of eighteen — about five feet, eight inches tall with long dark hair and brown eyes. I remember telling her that if only she had gone with Getzel to the Soviet Union maybe she could have had a chance at survival. Maybe she would have even married her boyfriend. She acknowledged that maybe she should have gone, but it was too late to do anything about it — and besides, at least she was here to help her younger brothers.

"We're all orphans now," she told us, as tears flowed down all our faces. "The future is so uncertain, but we have to continue to love each other even more. And we have to keep doing our best every day to survive." She told us to keep believing that better days would come and that she would do her best to help us survive.

Brenda had always been a big help to me. Not only had she provided me with her dress when I first started smuggling, but soon after that she helped me execute an extremely effective smuggling tactic using the streetcar.

There was a streetcar for gentiles that went through a small portion of the ghetto to quickly get from one "Aryan" street to another. It never stopped in the ghetto — there was no way Jews were going to be allowed on the vehicle. Nonetheless, I found a way to take advantage of the situation.

After crossing to the "Aryan" side and collecting a bag full of goods, I would go to the end of the line to get on that streetcar. I would stand right next to the conductor — whom I had bribed to ignore my smuggling — keeping the bag at my feet. It was shielded from view to all but the conductor. Sometimes there was a Polish policeman on the streetcar, but he was busy at the back making sure no one jumped on.

My sister would be waiting at a certain spot in the ghetto along the streetcar path. All the conductor had to do was unlock the door next to me as we approached my sister's location. No one saw anything as I would inconspicuously kick my bag out to her.

Most often, the streetcar was moving slowly enough that after I kicked the goods out, my sister had enough time to toss me an empty bag with a list telling me what to get next. I made at least four of these trips a day. The conductor took a great risk for us, but I made it worth his while by giving him a large portion of the profit. When I first came up with the idea, I carefully made my sales pitch to a couple of streetcar conductors, but could only convince the one to assist me. Fortunately, he was all I needed.

This scheme went on for a month or two, but in March 1941 the Germans changed the streetcar route and that was the end of it. But it was wonderful while it lasted, and I remember my mother being particularly proud of our ingenuity.

After the loss of my mom, it was back to my regular grind — smuggling for survival. As long as our eyes were open, our stomachs required food. Unfortunately, not long after returning to my routine, I had a scary incident that put me out of commission for quite a while. I was riding on the tail end of a streetcar one afternoon when I noticed there was a German patrol stopping all the streetcars. I did not know whether they were looking for Jews or for a specific individual.

The streetcar I was on was about two hundred metres from where the checkpoint was set up, and I realized I had to get out of there fast.

However, the streetcar was still moving at top speed. I had no choice — I jumped off and ran for my life. A German saw what I was doing, reached for his rifle and started to shoot at me.

I ran as fast as I could to the first available opening — a lane between two buildings. A few moments later I ran through to another street, which I crossed. As I was running, I crossed over some railway tracks, but my foot got caught in them and I tumbled down — striking my left knee hard on the metal and slicing it wide open. The wound began to bleed profusely, but I kept running for a few more minutes and somehow lost the Germans.

I got to a store where I purchased some superficial medical supplies: gauze and rubber bandages. What I really needed was treatment at a hospital — with stitches and real medicine. But I was too scared to go there. I didn't have any identification, and the hospital workers would ask all kinds of questions about why my parents weren't with me and how it happened.

Taking my chances, I lay down for a while and applied pressure to the cut area to stop the bleeding. As soon as I pulled my hand away, it started to bleed again. I quickly put a bandage on anyway and managed to drag myself through the ghetto wall and went straight home to get off my feet.

When I eventually changed the bandage and inspected the knee, I saw that it was full of puss. It was already infected and hurt like hell. I replaced the bandage with ointment and gauze, wrapped a couple more bandages around it and hoped for the best. For the next several days, I had a difficult time and stayed off my left leg as much as possible. It took almost a year to completely heal. To this day, there is a distinctive red scar on my knee as a reminder of that incident.

That recovery probably wouldn't have taken as long if I hadn't done so much damage to my knees in the prior year of smuggling. Many times I had to scale the ghetto wall and jump to the ground. Often, I was weighed down with goods. This took its toll on my knees, and a doctor in the ghetto even told me I had retained a lot of water in my knees and I would do serious damage if I didn't rest for a while. If I had taken his advice, we'd have starved to death.

With this new knee injury, however, I couldn't operate as I had with full mobility, so I had to turn to less physical tactics: I began begging. Although it was less lucrative, begging was much better than doing nothing. I put my cross around my neck and started to sing in front of apartment buildings where the richer people lived outside the ghetto. Sometimes I sang religious songs so no one would suspect that I was not a Christian. And I always made sure my hair was cut short and straight to conceal my naturally curly head of hair, which was rare for gentiles. I was also confident no one would suspect my Jewish identity because there were many Polish women and children who were so poor they too were begging.

Whenever I sang, people would throw down some bread or a few pennies. Occasionally, someone would even call me up and give me a plate of home-cooked food. What a treat that was. Usually, however, I returned home with a hoarse voice, a little cash and a bag filled with bread, potatoes and cabbage. Each evening Brenda would make soup, and we had a hearty meal — considering the conditions that surrounded us.

Although I managed to handle the day-to-day life of crossing the wall, Menashe had a more difficult time. He did courageously try to shoulder the smuggling burden alone while I recovered from my knee injury. It was too bad that he wasn't well suited for the work. He had more than his share of travails.

One of his scariest moments came one afternoon as he was approaching the ghetto wall with a large bag of potatoes on his back. Some gentile children were hanging around on the "Aryan" side. These individuals, known as shmaltzers,[1] used to know what the

---

1 A reference to the word *szmalcownik*, which comes from the Polish word *szmalec*, meaning "lard," and is a pejorative slang term for blackmailers who denounced Jews to the Gestapo, usually in exchange for money. The usage here possibly blends this term with *schmaltz*, Yiddish for chicken fat.

Jewish kids were doing and would try to steal from us as we came close to the wall. We had to be both careful and lucky to avoid them, though it was better to be confronted by a few shmaltzers than to face a German guard.

When several of these hoodlums demanded money from Menashe, he told them he didn't have any. One of the boys pulled out a knife and lunged forward, jabbing the knife toward the sack Menashe was carrying. The boy was trying to rip open the bag so all the potatoes would fall out. Sensing the attack, Menashe quickly turned around and took the swipe of the blade with his hand. Bleeding profusely, he ran from them and made it back through the wall — without losing any potatoes. We took him to a Jewish doctor, who stitched the wound for the payment of two potatoes.

Shortly after that incident, however, Menashe came home with a high fever and stomach pains. He had contracted typhus, which was rampant in the ghetto in the fall of 1941. Between that and his hand, it was the end of his smuggling for a while. About a week later, I came down with the disease too.

Typhus causes a person's temperature to shoot way up, they get chills, severe weakness, pains in their limbs and severe headaches. Hallucinations are also typical. On about the fourth or fifth day, a skin rash appears, which spreads throughout the body.

Typhus was deadly for thousands of Jews in the ghetto. We had no way to treat it and simply had to hope for the best from our immune system.

Now that Menashe and I were both flat on our backs, we had a problem. Even if we survived, how were we all going to eat? Fortunately, I had planned ahead in case something like this happened. Some of my smuggling days were extremely profitable. On those occasions, I put away some of the money as insurance. Without telling anyone, I hid the cash in the cuffs of my pants.

While we were ill, I told my sister not to worry too much because I had saved some money. She didn't believe me at first. She thought

I was babbling nonsense as a result of my fever. I had to convince her to hand me my pants to prove it. I reached in and pulled out five hundred złotys. It wasn't a fortune, but it was enough to keep us going until I recovered. She literally jumped for joy at the sight. She wanted to kiss me but realized that wasn't a good idea if she wanted to avoid being infected with the disease!

Menashe and I both recovered, although we were severely weakened after two precarious weeks on what at times felt like our death beds. We were lucky that Brenda and my little brother Eli didn't catch the disease.

After a couple of weeks of illness, we ran out of the money I had saved. I was not fully recovered — either from the typhus or my knee — but we desperately needed income again. I felt I was strong enough to return to my regular routine of crossing over to the "Aryan" side. Menashe did the same, while Brenda stayed home with Eli.

The next crisis struck in early spring 1942. Brenda now became seriously ill with an infection and was rushed to the ghetto's hospital. It wasn't a typical hospital and lacked both medicine and food. It was up to relatives to come and feed the patients. So when I visited her each afternoon, I would bring buttered bread and the occasional apple or pear.

With the burden already becoming heavier, we were dealt another blow shortly after Brenda entered the hospital. Menashe had been caught trying to smuggle food into the ghetto and was put in the prison at 24 Gęsia Street in the ghetto. The site, which consisted of adjoined structures, had previously served as a Polish military prison. In May 1942, there were about 1,300 Jews detained in the jail. All of the inmates suffered from starvation and were close to collapsing. Hundreds of the prisoners were children, most of whom had been caught smuggling, and these children were kept in a separate section.

I was able to get away with claiming to be eight years old in order to receive lenient treatment from the authorities because I looked so young. Menashe couldn't. He was a tall thirteen-year-old who looked older than his age. Though he was lucky to not be killed, he was held indefinitely, which was, in effect, a death sentence anyway because they gave the inmates virtually no food. The only way to help him survive was to bribe a guard to take some food to him. That put an extra strain on me. I now had two siblings to deliver food to — one in hospital and one in jail.

I didn't want to tell Brenda that Menashe was caught. I was afraid it would upset her and she would become sicker. I told her he had a bad cold and didn't want to visit for fear of worsening her illness. I delayed telling the truth as long as I could — until I was sure she was strong enough to handle the bad news.

I was now alone at home with Eli, and it was extremely difficult for both of us. I was constantly on the go — begging on the "Aryan" side and running back and forth between the jail and the hospital. Sensing the gravity of the situation, precocious Eli insisted on helping me. He figured we could double our income, and I decided we had little choice but to give it a try.

We continued with the singing and begging tactics I had recently initiated, and spent most of our time doing it together. Sometimes we'd jump on streetcars as they were loading up at the main terminal. As we begged, people would toss spare change into our hats. We sang Polish songs on street corners. After we'd accumulated enough złotys to buy a decent amount of food, we would smuggle that into the ghetto and distribute it to both Brenda and Menashe. This had to be done every day.

I remember one of those mornings leaving the ghetto when little Eli received quite a scare. As he was squeezing his way through a hole in the wall, a Polish policeman was standing off to the side waiting for him. Eli poked his arms and head out of the hole and was scanning for guards when the policeman suddenly grabbed him and repeatedly struck his head and hands with a stick. Eli screamed and cried and frantically yelled for me to pull him back in. I managed to, but he didn't come away unscathed. His blue eyes were nearly obscured by the black bruising around them, his head was swollen and tenderly sore, and he couldn't move his hands properly for weeks. Had it gone on much longer, I think he would have been beaten to death. The incident greatly frightened Eli, but he was remarkably tough and didn't let it deter him from smuggling. From then on, however, he would only climb the wall, never trusting the holes. He was an agile little guy; it was a ten-foot climb up the wall, and the only way to get down on the other side was to jump.

After a few more weeks, we received the excellent news that Brenda was to be released. When she left the hospital, I told her about Menashe. She was shocked and upset, but she also realized there was nothing she could do. Her immediate task was to take care of Eli and me, assuming the role of both mother and father. Even during such difficult times, she maintained a sense of optimism. However, circumstances were still to get much worse, and it wouldn't be long until optimism became all but impossible.

Hiding Out

Despite everything the Germans had done, their plan to systematically murder us in gas chambers was beyond our imagination. We had hoped their battles with the Soviets would eventually lead to the realization that Jews could be an exploitable resource for the war effort. So in the spring of 1942, when rumours started to circulate that the Germans were going to move everyone out of the ghetto, we figured they wanted to put us to work in places like armament factories.

One afternoon, there was talk on the street that early the next day the Germans were going to enter the ghetto to collect people. My sister felt it was best for Eli and me to leave the ghetto that night and permanently stay on the "Aryan" side. She said that if there was a door-to-door roundup, she had a better chance of surviving because she was a young, energetic woman who could be used as labour, whereas we were just expendable little kids. She reminded us that neither of us had Jewish appearances and we had the street smarts to survive on the outside.

I didn't like the idea of separating and told her we would only go if she came with us.

"You go first," she responded. "You can get established over there and then I'll follow. You can adapt better there. As little kids, you can sleep anywhere and can always beg for food." She insisted that we listen to her because she was the oldest remaining child and was doing what my parents would have wanted.

As a compromise, I said I would go if she allowed me to return to check on her every couple of days — and to bring food and money to her. She agreed to that, and the discussion was over. The rest of the day we quietly got ourselves organized to leave that night.

Just before we left, the silence was broken when Brenda could no longer hold back her tears. "What have they done to our family?" she asked rhetorically. Eli and I started to cry as well, and we embraced her, trying to console each other by saying that everything would turn out okay. I promised her that I would take good care of Eli.

We had to be extremely cautious as we left the ghetto. The guards worked rotating eight-hour shifts to ensure twenty-four-hour surveillance. I picked the part of the wall adjacent to the market, hoping the market stalls would provide hiding places that were only a short distance from the ghetto.

After getting to the top of the wall, we looked around carefully and didn't see any German soldiers or Polish police. We jumped down to the other side, and scrambled into the market area. We hid among the stalls and prayed for the best. After our hearts slowed down and we felt comfortable that no one was around, we drifted off to sleep for the night. We couldn't go anywhere because any Pole caught outdoors after the 9:00 p.m. curfew could be shot.

Unfortunately, we slept for a little longer than we would have liked and were still asleep at dawn when the curfew ended. We were awakened by the woman who owned the stall we were in. "Jesus Christ, you nearly gave me a heart attack," she yelled out. "Who the hell are you? What are you doing here?"

Startled and acting on instinct, we yelled back — telling her that we were poor kids who had run away from home because our father beat us up. We said we needed a place to sleep and her booth was the right place at the right time.

As we got to our feet we calmed down. We thanked her and apologized for the inconvenience. That seemed to soften her demeanour, and as we readied to leave she gave each of us a piece of fresh bread. We were starving, so we really appreciated the gesture.

We were off to a good start. We hopped onto a streetcar that took us over to Grochowska Street — a place where we had had a lot of success begging and singing. More importantly, it was where Mr. and Mrs. Slawcia had their little cafe.

I explained our predicament and asked if my little brother and I could stay in their restaurant until the tension in the ghetto subsided. They agreed to take us in. They knew we were Jewish and that they could be given the death penalty if caught hiding us — but they helped us anyway. I trusted them completely, and it gave me peace of mind to know we were safe there at night.

To minimize the risk to the Slawcias, we would stay on the streets until just before curfew. We also needed the full day to acquire the money and food required for our siblings' survival. Sometimes Eli and I would work together; other times we would split up and I would go back to the ghetto. I always went alone because I felt that if there was a German attack while I was in the ghetto at least Eli would survive.

The Germans didn't liquidate the ghetto as the rumours had suggested, nor did they over the next few days, so I delivered food to Menashe and Brenda. I also made some extra money by carrying messages from adult smugglers on the "Aryan" side to their colleagues in the ghetto. What's more, I took some additional groceries into the ghetto, which I exchanged for clothing, which I would sell outside the ghetto to make even more money.

When I met up with Brenda we hugged with joy, relieved to see each other again. "How is Eli?" she asked. "I miss him so much. How I long to hold him close to me."

I told her how I kept a close watch on him as he spent his day singing songs at the streetcar stand across the street from where I would kneel down and beg. He was well-suited for the work — he looked even more "Aryan" than me, with blond hair and a small, upturned nose. He also spoke excellent Polish and could handle the physical rigours, since he was larger and taller than me, despite our age difference.

I told Brenda that he had quickly become accustomed to life on the "Aryan" side and was earning more than his share on the streets. When we compared who had made more money at the end of each day, he beat me every time. And that didn't take into account the occasional sandwich he used to be given — something that happened to me much less frequently.

Brenda smiled as she listened to the update and asked if I could bring Eli with me for a visit. I said I would do my best.

Three days later the Germans still hadn't started with any round-ups, so I did bring Eli into the ghetto. He too had been asking me each day when he'd be able to see his sister again, so when the opportunity came he was excited. It was a heartening visit — a few moments of happiness before our world was turned upside down yet again.

~

All of the rumours that had been circulating eventually came true. On July 19, 1942 — unknown to us at the time — the Germans had ordered the mass deportation of Polish Jews, including those in the Warsaw ghetto, to the killing centres and other camps by the end of the year. Intense efforts to start the process began just a few days later. Starting on July 22, thousands of Jews per day were taken from the ghetto to the gas chambers of the Treblinka killing centre, which commenced operations on July 23.

I was in the ghetto on the morning of July 22 visiting some smuggling friends after seeing my sister. When my friends noticed that troops were gathering around the ghetto, they suggested it would be best that I remain with them.

By nine o'clock in the morning, German SS and police units, as well as German auxiliaries made up of Soviet prisoners of war (Lithuanians, Latvians and Ukrainians), had surrounded the ghetto, while several trucks had entered to collect Jews. The Jewish ghetto police, originally reporting to the Judenrat (the Jewish Council who administered the ghetto), did much of the dirty work under the watchful eyes of the Germans in charge.

All entrances and exits to dwellings would be blocked and tenants ordered to come out, present their documents and be prepared to leave. The Jewish police inspected the apartments to make sure all the inhabitants had complied with the order. We could discern no pattern as to which houses were being selected.

Most people thought they were just being sent to a labour camp, so they voluntarily marched off. They were told the roundups were for a "resettlement in the East." Each deportee was permitted to take along some luggage and all their valuables.

These people were then taken to the *Umschlagplatz* — a large yard at the edge of the ghetto that merged into the railway tracks and bordered on the hospital Brenda had stayed in. The hospital had been evacuated and converted into an overly cramped, filthy holding area for the train platform.

The unlucky souls to be "resettled" were moved from the hospital to the *Umschlagplatz* and then into enclosed cattle trains. They crammed over a hundred men, women and children into those cattle cars. Without food, water or ventilation, the conditions were terrible — even for cattle. As a result, the many that were weak died in transit.

Those who survived the trip to Treblinka were told upon arrival to take a shower, after which they would be fed. They were stripped and taken into large rooms. Instead of showers, however, the doors were locked and poison gas was piped into the rooms. It only took a few minutes to kill scores of people — disgustingly efficient and sadistic. The bodies were inspected, and gold tooth fillings were extracted and set aside before the flesh and bones were turned to ashes in crematoria. The camps were death factories.

~

My adult friends were about to transform themselves from smugglers to freedom fighters. They were not naive — they knew not to believe a word of the German propaganda. These friends insisted that we keep a low profile until the Germans relented. Fortunately, the Germans stayed away from the houses on our street. Nonetheless, we didn't take any chances. The smuggling leaders were the only ones who ventured outside to occasionally get us food and water.

With such tight security around the ghetto walls — and the risk of being taken away if I wandered onto the wrong street at the wrong time — I realized there was no option but to stay put and let the adults take the risks. I could only hope that my sister was staying hidden too. I felt reasonably assured that Eli was safe on the outside, but I was worried sick about Menashe. Jail was not the place to be under such circumstances.

With nowhere to go, I spent a lot of time getting close to the dozen or so people in our apartment. There was a couple there I particularly liked named Joe and Chawa. They had a two-year-old daughter named Schajadala. Knowing how bad things were and to give the child a chance to survive, the couple had recently given their daughter to a gentile family who lived on a farm. The farmers were well paid to take care of Schajadala; the deal was that if either birth parent survived the war, they would be able to get the child back.

Chawa was a nervous wreck and had tears in her eyes all day long. Joe kept his emotions more to himself, but it was obvious by the pain on his face that he was devastated too. They were full of guilt over what they had done but were only thinking of their child's welfare. They just wanted her to have the chance to grow up and have a decent life. I think they made the right decision, since survival in the ghetto in the summer of 1942 seemed impossible.

By the last few days of July, while I remained in hiding with Joe, Chawa and the others, people in the ghetto began to figure out what the Germans were up to and stopped handing themselves over voluntarily. Stories filtered back to the ghetto about what was happening at the camps. Those few who managed to escape told us that people there had virtually no chance of survival. One of our leaders told a story about a father who was given labour duty to stave off death for a few days — his job was to shove dead bodies into the ovens, including his own family.

With less cooperation from their victims, the Germans and their auxiliaries became more active, doing more of the work themselves and more forcefully directing the Jewish police. Deportations became increasingly haphazard and unpredictable. People were dragged away from their homes without their bags. To try to get more volunteers to come to the *Umschlagplatz*, the Nazis enticed people with bread and marmalade. Some people were so hungry they went for it, even realizing it meant probable death.

The soldiers also began grabbing more people randomly off the street and initiating extremely aggressive housing raids. That's when things got difficult for us. One morning, after I had been in our apartment for nearly a week, we were woken up by a warning.

"Get up, get up," we were told in a panic. "The Germans have entered the ghetto in massive numbers! They're going to raid all the buildings."

We got dressed quickly and rushed via a network of connections from rooftop to rooftop to a hiding place at 17 Wołyńska Street, which had been prepared for such an occasion. It was a much larger, better-hidden place than the apartment we had been staying in.

There were about seventy of us in that attic. Everyone was scared, but for the most part managed to remain calm. Late in the morning, we heard the Germans roam around the staircase beneath us. Somehow, they never found us. We had survived for the moment.

We were among the fortunate. With the help of the traitorous ghetto police, the Nazis hauled off many more Jews than on any of the previous days. All I could think about was my sister. Where was she hiding during these apartment raids? I wanted to rush over to her place, but Joe held me back. He said I would likely get caught by the Germans and that would be the end of me.

"But what about my sister?" I kept repeating. "She is all alone right now worrying about me. I'm safe here, but I have no idea what's happened to her."

Still, he was wisely persistent in not letting me go.

"She is probably hiding too," he said. "You'd never find her."

I respected and admired Joe so much I felt compelled to listen to him. During the discussion, he said to me: "You will survive if you are destined to. It's the same for your sister. Just hang in there as best you can and let destiny take its course."

He was stoic about everything. In our new hiding place, we talked more about his daughter, and he said he had accepted the reality that he would never have the joy of seeing her grow up. He knew he wasn't going to survive the war and insisted he wasn't going to die quietly when his time came. I found such talk inspirational.

By nightfall, after the Germans had gathered the day's sizable capture of Jews, the liquidation was temporarily suspended from our area. Some of the men left the hiding place in search of food and to find out what happened to some of their friends. I went with them, and while I had the opportunity, dashed over to my sister's place to see if she was okay.

There were a few people milling about in front of her building. They were from the building next door and had managed to get by undetected. They told me that when Brenda's building had been raided she was taken away along with about twenty others.

I felt my heart sink to the ground with crushing sadness. And before I had time to fully absorb the blow, I got hit with more bad news.

The Gęsia prison housing Menashe was close by, so I asked the group if they knew what the situation was there. They said the prison had been emptied a few days ago and that all the boys and girls had been shipped off. The Germans' barbarism was incomprehensible — all the beautiful little children had been ruthlessly murdered. Menashe was one of these poor victims — part of the first groups to be gassed at Treblinka at the start of the mass killings.

Menashe and Brenda were now gone. I cried and cried, oblivious to the people around me. I vomited what little food was in my gut and ran to our hiding place.

In the midst of my crying, I told the tragedy that besieged me to everyone else in the attic. People tried to comfort me, telling me not to give up hope. By that point I was numb — I knew I'd never see my lovely sister and dear brother again. There are no words to describe the pain I felt that night.

I only managed to keep from breaking down completely because there wasn't time to think. I just wanted to get the hell out of the ghetto and be with my one remaining sibling — my brother Eli who was still on the "Aryan" side. I didn't feel safe in the ghetto. The Germans didn't discover us this time, but that didn't mean we would be so lucky tomorrow. The next morning, I decided to move.

The only people the Germans did not round up were a relative few Jewish labourers with special passes. The Nazis had figured it was best to get what they could out of the healthiest Jews before killing them. Each day the workers would leave for their slave duty on the outside. I decided they would be my vehicle out. A friend in the hideout told me where a group of these workers gathered each morning.

I saw a group there of about a hundred to two hundred young and strong Jewish men beginning to congregate. As the men waited for the Germans to arrive, I talked to a couple who confirmed that they were going to work on the "Aryan" side. I asked if I could join them as a way to get out of the ghetto. They told me I was too small and that if the Germans spotted me they would immediately shoot me. They said I was crazy.

But they didn't say no. Having just lost my brother and sister, I didn't care. I was either going to see my little brother or die.

As I marched with the men, I somehow remained inconspicuous. I was so small I was tough to spot among all the big bodies. And I was lucky that these Jews helped me — doing their best to shield me from the Germans' view. I took off as soon as we passed through the gate to the "Aryan" side, running as fast as I could. I still don't know how I made it — total luck, I suppose, that there were only a couple of Germans guarding that whole group of men.

I jumped on the tail of a streetcar going to Praga, and went down to Grochowska Street, where my little brother was staying. As soon as I walked in the door, I leaped into his arms. I was so happy to see that he was fine, and he was relieved to see that I was alive.

Eli and I clung to one another — all we had now was each other. The Slawcias were also happy to see me. They said they thought they'd never see me alive again. In a brief moment of morbid levity, I told them I was a cat with nine lives and that I still had a couple more to use up.

Once the warmth of our exchange wore off, I told Eli about Brenda and Menashe. It took a moment or two until the reality hit him. We sobbed for several minutes before he spoke: "If it's just you and me who are left out of our entire family, which one of us is next?"

I assured him that I would look out for him and that we would both make it. We would survive the war, I said, and have some great times together in the years to come. We hugged again with tears in our eyes.

A few days later, as we were feeling extremely depressed and still grieving our loss, we had a particularly good day on the streets. That evening, I said we should get something good to eat as a way to lift our spirits. My brother suggested having a small glass of whisky. It seemed he had been exposed to the cafe's famous drink while I had been away. He really did have a mischievous side to him. I had already caught him smoking a cigarette once. He had had an entire pack and some matches in his pocket. I gave him hell for it.

This time the drinking led to a new lecture from me.

"You're only nine years old," I said. "Why are you going to drink booze at such a young age? A glass of milk would be more appropriate."

He said that one time when I was away, Mrs. Slawcia had given him a shot of whisky with some pepper in it to calm his upset stomach. I told him that didn't make it right — and that he'd better promise never to smoke or drink — "or else."

"Or else what?" he asked.

"Or else I'll have nothing to do with you anymore," I replied.

"You must be kidding," he said. "You smoke. And I've seen you drink."

"You are only nine years old. I am eleven. When you get to be my age, I'll let you smoke and drink too," I said facetiously as we both smiled. Then a look of concern came over his face.

"What if I don't make it to eleven?" he asked.

"Don't talk like that," I snapped back. "You must have a more positive attitude. We will both survive the war and have great lives when this is all over. You'll see."

He smiled again and hugged me. He also promised not to smoke or drink. And to the best of my knowledge, he kept that promise.

~

As the liquidation of the ghetto continued, I survived on the "Aryan" streets with Eli. It was bewildering to hear about the atrocities taking place in the ghetto. I didn't know what to think anymore. On the one hand, now that I knew the Germans' plan to murder the Jews, I promised myself that I would never be taken alive; I vowed never to allow them to ship me to the gas chambers. Dying was acceptable, provided I died with a purpose. I just wanted revenge — a chance to be able to fight back in some way.

I could not comprehend why for so long we Jews hadn't organized ourselves more and obtained weapons to fight for our murdered parents, brothers and sisters. We already had one cheek slapped and now we were turning our face so the other side could be smacked as well. If only I were an adult, I thought, I could organize some resistance. I visualized myself dying heroically in battle.

On the other hand — and the part of me that eventually prevailed — I really wanted to live, to see the Nazi regime pay for what it had done. I kept telling Eli that we would survive, that one day we would get married and be the seeds replenishing the Klajman family. "The tree will grow like wildfire," I would tell him.

That is not to say that we weren't realistic. We figured there was maybe a one-in-a-hundred chance of survival, but that was good enough for hope. As my smuggler friend Joe told me: "Where there is hope there is life, and where there is life there is hope."

I thought it was a great phrase, and I kept repeating it to Eli. "Have hope, we must have hope. Every day of survival is one more day of hope."

Eli and I were a great team — two brothers who both loved one another and got along like best friends.

Often, on days when we didn't do well begging, we had no choice but to steal food to survive. In the summer and early fall, I stole from the twice-weekly farmers' market. I took turnips, apples, carrots — whatever was easiest at that moment. I remember many autumn breakfasts of cold turnip.

Eli, on the other hand, was much better at the game than me. He never chose the easiest picking. He went for what he wanted most — and that wasn't turnip. He wanted to steal fresh bread and baked goods.

I could never figure out how Eli did it. No matter how carefully the food was guarded, he always seemed to get his hands on what he was after. And it wasn't often that he was caught. Only occasionally would he get over-anxious and make himself conspicuous when he grabbed an item. And even then, he was always quick enough to get away.

One time he was caught stealing a loaf of bread. As he scrambled off, the merchant ran up to him and gave him a hard kick in the butt. As soon as Eli met up with me an hour later, the first thing he did was kick me in the behind.

"You said we should share everything 50/50. Well, that's your half," he said. We both laughed as we enjoyed the bread.

Between the two of us, we were making enough to eat every day. The only problem was where to sleep at night. We had a safe place every night at Mr. and Mrs. Slawcia's cafe until a grease fire in August destroyed their place. They weren't harmed but they lost everything they owned and had to move to the countryside to stay with relatives.

Shelter wasn't as vital in the summer as in winter. On clear nights, we could sleep in the cornfields or in the park among the large, dense trees. One priority we had was to stay clean, and that was one advantage to the park; it bordered on the Vistula River, so we could wash ourselves and our clothes in the river. We cleaned ourselves for health reasons and for security. If we were too dirty, we could give ourselves away.

We still needed to find shelter on rainy nights, which could be a problem. The first couple of wet nights were terrifying. We managed to find a couple of apartment attics, but that was risky. We could easily be caught and turned over, and it was unwise to stay in the same place twice, which could arouse suspicion.

One afternoon we stumbled across an idea that solved our problem. I saw a large piece of land where vegetables were growing. After we stole a few tomatoes, a man who spotted our theft started chasing us. We got away easily, and he didn't see enough of us to recognize us later.

The man had come out of a shed adjacent to the field. He was a night watchman paid to make sure people like us or other criminals didn't steal any produce. The shed looked like it would offer protection — that man was the only person in sight for quite a distance.

It was obvious he wasn't making much money working seven nights a week for a rich tomato grower. So I offered him rent if he'd let us stay in the shed on rainy nights. He was all for the idea — it was extra money for which he didn't have to do anything. Plus, he felt good about doing it — helping two boys he thought were Christian orphans.

We told him that our father was an alcoholic who beat us every day and also beat our mother, who fled one day with another man because she could no longer tolerate the abuse. We said we didn't like the boyfriend and had made her choose between him and us — she chose him. We explained that we had no option but to run away, and it was up to me to take care of little "Wiesrek" — our Polish name for Eli, just as my Polish alias was Janek. After we told the watchman our story, he took great pity on us. He would often give us soup and sometimes even let us stay for free.

Back in the ghetto, the Germans stopped their daily collection of Jews in mid-September. By that point, almost 300,000 Jews — the vast majority of the total ghetto population — had been sent to be murdered.

I had been on the outside for nearly two months, so I was curious about the ghetto and felt compelled to return. I still had lots of unanswered questions, including what had happened to the people I was with — particularly my friend Joe, who had so graciously taken me under his wing in that hiding spot. I was also anxious to make some money. Ghetto smuggling paid far more handsomely than begging, and with the *Aktionen*, the roundups, over it seemed possible to return.

Having spent these past weeks with Eli, I was pleased with how well he was doing under such difficult circumstances. I felt he was tough enough to be left on his own while I went to the ghetto. When I said I was going to take a day or two away from him, his first reaction was fear. He was worried I would never return and he'd be left abandoned.

I explained that it really was necessary that I go — not just to check up on my friends, but as a way to make some much-needed money. He didn't like the idea but understood my reasons and told me to hurry back as soon as I could.

That autumn day, I slipped into the ghetto through a hole in the wall.

Back to the Ghetto

It was a Friday, and I had brought some fish with me to sell for the Sabbath dinner. By this point, there weren't that many people left in the ghetto, and even fewer who could afford to pay for the food. But I found them. I exchanged the food for clothing, the only article of value left in the ghetto. I felt sorry for these people, but at least they were lucky enough to be able to eat when so many others had died.

I used the rest of my time in the ghetto to determine what had happened to those who had been hiding with me at the beginning of the *Aktion* — especially Joe. Through a contact on the "Aryan" side, I arranged a rendezvous with a few surviving smuggling friends who were now in the Jewish underground. These men had been friends with Joe.

They told me that Joe had been rounded up to be taken to Treblinka just like all the others. Other than me, the smuggling leaders who had been out getting food at the time of the raid were the only survivors from the group.

Joe had said he would do something to fight back when captured, and he kept his word. Just before turning himself in to be taken away, he hid a large pair of pincers in his shirt. I suspect he may have thought he'd be able to cut through the fence of the camp to escape, but maybe he just wanted a weapon.

Whatever his motive, when Joe got to the *Umschlagplatz* he had apparently been verbally abused by a German officer. Joe reacted by pulling out the pincers and jumping on the officer — cutting his throat and digging in — refusing to let go.

Joe was about thirty-five years of age and one of the biggest and strongest men I knew. He kept digging deeper and deeper into the Nazi's throat, even as several Germans pumped round after round of ammunition into his possessed body. He died still firmly gripping the pincers, which had long ago killed the Gestapo man. He had ripped his throat to pieces.

To me, he was the greatest hero in the world. People talked about his courage for months after that incident. Although he fell to the ground as another dead Jew, he had taken a German with him. He was a valiant martyr. Perhaps more than any other individual in the war, he was the most inspirational to me. I am proud to have known him and proud to have considered him my friend and idol.

I believe his wife was loaded onto a train and murdered at Treblinka. I do not know what became of their daughter, whom they had sent away. I assume she married a Pole and lived the life of a gentile — never knowing her true heritage. I had asked Joe and Chawa to tell me where Schajadala was. I thought that if I survived the war and they didn't, I could find their daughter and pass on the truth of her past. But they refused to give me the information, fearing that if I was captured and tortured I might reveal the story.

This trip to the ghetto brought me nothing but sad news. Almost all of my smuggling friends who were my age had been taken to Treblinka. All the older friends I had made were gone too. I felt overcome with bitter hatred. I hated the Germans, I hated the Poles and I hated the Jews who collaborated with the Nazis when they came in to round us up.

I couldn't understand how a civilized nation like Germany could do such unthinkable things. And what about many of the Poles? There were some brave ones who helped us, but many were indifferent to our plight and sometimes just as bad or even worse than the Germans. Worst of all, I couldn't believe there were Jews who thought they might survive by turning in other Jews. Those who helped the Germans were given better rations, but ultimately they too were shipped to camps and gassed alongside those they betrayed.

I just wanted to get out of there and return to my brother. I slipped through the wall and made it to Grochowska Street before curfew. When I greeted Eli, he was just as excited and relieved to see me as the night the *Aktion* began.

"Eli, don't worry about me," I joked with him. "I'm indestructible. I'm on a mission to get both of us to survive this rotten war."

As September gave way to October, our farm shed haven was locked up for the season. We were back to the daily search for shelter during fall and winter. We made hiding places out of basements, attics or whatever other small spaces were available in apartment buildings. We would take straw mats that people left out in front of their apartment doors and use them as mattresses. An empty potato bag was our blanket. We both climbed inside and slept close to one another to gain the benefit of maximum shared body heat.

Our nomadic existence was both risky and stressful. Following the *Aktion*, the Germans were aware that some Jews had escaped the ghetto and were living clandestinely on the "Aryan" side. To weed us out, they used a carrot-and-stick approach with the Poles. The death penalty had been decreed for any Pole found helping to hide a Jew, but they also offered rewards, usually five hundred złotys or three kilograms of sugar, to any Poles who turned a Jew over to the authorities. There were posters everywhere announcing these rewards. Unfortunately, many Poles seized the opportunity.

To avoid being caught by Germans or the Poles they bribed, we slept in different places every night. Even when begging and singing, we didn't stay in one place for too long. It didn't matter if we were really successful in a particular spot; we had to move around regularly so no one got too suspicious.

One day toward the end of 1942, Eli and I had just chosen a particular apartment block to sing in when two children approached us. Normally, we kept our distance from everyone to keep our identities secret, but occasionally we would chat — just so we didn't look too paranoid.

After just a few minutes of small talk with these two boys, they somehow must have figured out that we were Jews. Perhaps it was because they sensed we were in a similar predicament. In a rare and dangerous display of candour, they stunned us by telling us that they themselves were Jews. Once the shock wore off, we couldn't help but smile. It was great to know that someone else was going through the same experience as we were.

The boys' names were Zenek and Paweł. They were brothers who had been rounded up during the first liquidation but managed to get out of their train car on the way to Treblinka. They had brought some tools that enabled them to pry open the door.

They both jumped out of that moving train and were luckily unhurt. They got back to Warsaw but stayed out of the ghetto. They were like me in that they spoke good Polish and could pass as Christian boys.

There was also another boy we met in a similar manner. His name was Zbyszek. He was an independent-minded, strong character, a year or two older than me. He looked particularly "Aryan" and used this to great advantage, even finding work with a merchant in the market. As time went on, he became my closest friend. Our group of five often hung out together.

In early winter, when the choice of attics and basements became even more limited, Eli and I finally found somewhere to stay. It was an old horse stable in an area that had been rezoned for apartment buildings. We lived in a unit that still had hay on the ground. We had to pay rent — which wasn't expensive since it was a horse stable.

We never trusted the elderly couple who were our landlords the way we had trusted the Slawcias. We didn't dare say that we were

Jewish. And they never asked — knowing that ignorance was bliss if trouble ever arose. But it must have crossed their minds. Why else would two children be sleeping in horse hay?

Now that there was a safe place for Eli to sleep, I decided to once again smuggle full-time. He could beg on the "Aryan" side while I made larger sums with my adult friends. I needed extra money to be able to pay the rent. The additional income would also allow us to eat a lot better, and with the cold winter upon us it became even more important to be decently nourished.

Each trip back to the ghetto reinforced my bitterness. The Jews in the ghetto were faced with such a hostile environment that was only getting worse, and I kept asking myself why they couldn't fight back. Why did we have to be cowards, acting like sheep being sent to the slaughter? There had to be a way to put up some resistance.

The battle finally came — the only problem was that it was too little, too late.

∼

If God or no one else was going to stop the Germans, it was up to us to defend ourselves.

The last time I remembered Jews fighting in any meaningful way was before the war. There were often groups of Polish boys on the hunt for Jews, terrorizing us whenever the opportunity presented itself. Skirmishes were common.

One time, however, several of the tougher Jewish boys in my neighbourhood sought retaliation. Armed with knives and steel chains, these boys rented a horse-and-buggy and went over to the non-Jewish gangs' neighbourhoods. Using what could be called "commando" tactics, they gave the thugs a taste of their own medicine — teaching them that attacking us could result in painful consequences.

The *Aktion* that summer had completely changed the face of the ghetto. After that *Aktion*, there were only about 60,000 Jews remaining, spread out among three zones which were separated by large stretches of evacuated territory. There was the brushmakers' shops area, which contained a brush factory and other little shops, the little Többens's area — another enterprise zone, where Jews did forced labour in German factories — and the central ghetto. Jews were not allowed to move from one zone to another, but it wasn't strictly enforced so people moved around quite freely.

The temporary calm the Germans had created did not deceive us. Perhaps the devastation of the *Aktion* was the final straw, but people in the ghetto finally realized death was certain to come sooner or later and so they had nothing to lose by resisting.

With no fear of death, we were energized to fight to the best of our abilities. Everyone knew the chance of victory was zero, but winning wasn't the goal. We just wanted to die with dignity. This attitude gave me a sense of pride and satisfaction. It was wonderful to see everyone pull together with such great purpose. I knew that if any Jews in the country would stand up and fight, it would be Warsaw ghetto Jews.

To have any success, weapons had to be obtained. Much of our arsenal was homemade — most notably Molotov cocktails, small incendiary weapons made with glass bottles that could be thrown. The rest had to be purchased and smuggled into the ghetto, which was difficult, though not impossible. Jews in the ghetto obtained guns from Poles outside the ghetto, some of whom had hidden their weapons when the Germans took control of Poland in 1939. A few members of the Polish underground who worked in armament factories in and around Warsaw even managed to smuggle out some items, which they would sell to our fighters.

One of our biggest challenges was paying for the goods. Many thousands of złotys were needed. Guns cost twelve thousand złotys apiece, the price of a bullet was one hundred złotys and the cost of a grenade was ten thousand złotys. The young Jewish fighters — the de facto rulers of the ghetto — forcibly taxed everyone in the area to obtain the required funds, especially the remaining few who were rich (the major smugglers). Most of the jewellery, furs and other valuable items that remained hidden were poured into the effort.

To make matters even more difficult, any arms we purchased or acquired from the Polish underground still had to be smuggled into the ghetto. That's where my friends played a key role. Prior to the resistance they had just been food smugglers; now they were bringing arms in.

On January 18, 1943, the Germans marched in for their second *Aktion*. The ghetto was blockaded early in the morning. Then the German units and support troops penetrated. For the most part, the Jews still didn't have enough guns or ammunition to put up mass resistance. However, they put up resistance, and that was important because it was the first time the Germans had encountered any, and it was enough to keep them off balance. They were no longer marching into the ghetto with smiles on their faces expecting easy work.

What frustrated them most was that the Jews were hiding. For weeks, people had been gathering in hidden attics and cellars, and the Germans were hesitant to enter these for fear of being ambushed.

The Nazis had wanted to round up eight thousand people in a one-day effort. However, they only captured three thousand that first day but returned over the next few days when they could only catch two thousand more. They also killed about a thousand Jews in the streets — in retaliation for the Germans we killed or injured.

After the Nazis left the ghetto, we knew the fight had just begun and that they'd be back with increased force to finish off what remained of the Jews here. But we were going to be ready. The Nazis were going to have a battle on their hands if they wanted to send the rest of the about 60,000 Jews off to be murdered. We were going to make our mark in history.

From February to April 1943, the Jews in the ghetto focused on improving their hiding places. In January, Jews had generally concealed themselves in attics and cellars — improvised arrangements.

After the January *Aktion*, there was a concerted effort to build elaborate bunkers — subterranean shelters designed to sustain many people for long periods of time.

Throughout April, there were persistent rumours of a coming German incursion, and people were ready to go to their bunkers on a moment's notice. Most of this was taking place while I was on the "Aryan" side with my brother. However, I was still making frequent trips into the ghetto, so I was aware that the resistance efforts were underway. I was there for the most famous moment in the ghetto's history.

I was almost looking forward to the enemy coming into the ghetto. I had a sense that I would witness a historic day, which Jewish children would learn about for centuries to come.

I really didn't know much about the specifics of the resistance. The most important planning had been done in total secrecy; with my birthday approaching, I was not yet twelve, so from the fighters' perspective I didn't need to know much. But my smuggling life got me in close enough contact with some in the Jewish Combat Organization (the Żydowska Organizacja Bojowa, known as the ŻOB) that I had a sense of what was happening. I was enthusiastic to do whatever I could to help the cause and occasionally I was used as a messenger boy. I was sent from one section of the ghetto to another, delivering weapons to various groups.

Most of the fighters were young adults — I figure the whole group of them were in their twenties or early thirties. They were extremely impressive — heroic men and women ready to die with honour. The leader of the ŻOB was Mordecai Anielewicz, then only in his early twenties. He headquartered the movement from 18 Miła Street in the ghetto.

I never met Anielewicz, but there were four big-time fighters whom I had come to know quite well. They were among the ghetto's major smugglers — bringing wagons of food through the gates past guards they had bribed. Whenever I had to stay over in the ghetto, they fed me and let me sleep at their home — if you can call it that, because it consisted of little more than a few smelly mattresses and boxes. But it was safe there, and that was all that mattered.

I suppose you could say I was their pet. I would always bring them small treats they specifically asked for — usually specialty deli items, such as sausages.

Their names were Szlojme, Jacob, Aaron and Jankiel Kleinman — I remember his last name because of its similarity to mine. I admired him the most; he was a large man who was the leader of the gang. He was a rough-and-tumble character, but he had a big heart.

There were two women who stayed with them — Zlata and "Florida" — who did their cleaning and cooking and who were also their sex partners. I couldn't understand why they called the older woman Florida; when I asked one of the men, he told me they gave her that name because "a lot of ships sailed into her."

"Get the picture Jankiel?" he asked.

As a naive twelve-year-old, I wasn't quite sure what he meant, but I didn't want to look stupid, so I said I understood. I even remember telling him: "You don't have to draw me a picture to explain it."

That place was wild. In the daytime, they smuggled and slept. During the night, the men boozed heavily, played cards and did what they wanted with the women. And they didn't restrict themselves to only Zlata and Florida.

Whenever they tired of sex with Zlata and Florida, the men would send me out to a certain address with a note. I would wait a few minutes for a response, and every time the answer would be: "Yes, they will be there at the requested hour."

"They" were always pretty young women who would trade sex for food. This was what they had to do to survive. Requesting these other women insulted Zlata and Florida, who were even in the room when the men did this. But what were they to do? Zlata and Florida had no choice. Where would they stay? How would they eat?

I knew that the men's behaviour was inappropriate, but the

circumstances of the ghetto changed people. Because we were all certain we were going to die, we didn't care about anything but living life
as fully as we could; any of us could be dead in the next minute, hour
or day. I liked those men and learned a lot from them. Their influence made me a tougher person — they taught me how to confront
whatever hardship might come along.

I too was behaving in ways that were unheard of for a boy my age.
I drank my share of vodka, often passing out on the floor after a few
shots. I did not drink for the joy of it, but to block out the pain of my
existence.

Despite the misery, the anarchy of the situation did result in a few
good times too — the best of which involved Zlata. Right from the
start, she made quite an impression on me. In contrast to Florida, I
thought Zlata was a sophisticated and intellectual woman.

I was sick with a cold one night while staying in the men's apartment. Jankiel told me he had a sure cure for my ailment. When I
asked him what that was, he smiled and said I would soon find out.

I had just undressed to go to sleep when Jankiel, a little drunk
at that point in the night, picked me up off my mattress and took
me over to Zlata. Telling her to keep me warm and devise a remedy
for my cold, he pulled her blanket back and dropped me right on
top of her. She was nude and so was I. It was a bizarre scene, and I
didn't know how to react. I turned beet red, feeling extremely awk-
ward and shy lying flesh-to-flesh on top of this twenty-eight-year-
old woman.

I thought Zlata wouldn't be too keen on the idea, but she just
laughed and started cuddling me. After a few minutes, I began to
figure out what was going on; before I knew it, she had slid her hand
down into my groin. She asked me if I liked what she was doing.
After I told her I did, and she verified it by seeing I had an erection,
she laughed and remarked: "Jankala has an erection. Not bad for a
twelve-year-old."

She played with my penis for a while and then whispered in my ear: "Jankala, would you like to put it in my vagina? I know you are a young little virgin, but would you like to play like the big boys?"

"I thought you were just supposed to warm me up," I said, feeling intimidated by this older, beautiful woman.

"Do you not find me attractive enough?" she wondered.

I told her she was very pretty.

"Don't you think this is weird?" I asked, remarking on our age difference.

"Sooner or later," she replied, "you will be with a woman, so why not now? I can feel you seem capable. And you're not feeling well, so this might make you feel better."

Before I knew it, I had lost my virginity. I didn't know what to think.

After I was finished, I went to the end of the mattress and Jankiel had sex with her for the rest of the evening as I watched.

Jankiel asked me afterwards if his treatment idea had helped my cold. He said that it was probably "better than chicken soup." Sheepishly, I nodded in agreement.

The following morning, I asked Zlata why she had had sex with me. She said there were two reasons. "Reason number one is because Mr. Jankiel asked me to," she said. "And I always do what Mr. Jankiel asks. But more importantly, reason number two is that I wanted to introduce you to sex. You deserve to experience the feel of a woman because there's a good chance you'll die before you reach adulthood. You might even die tomorrow, so you should enjoy the warmth of a woman if only once in your young life."

I told her I understood what she meant — and that she was as wise as she was beautiful. I asked her why I always had to bring other women when the men already had her and Florida. "Doesn't that upset you?" I asked.

"They like variety," she said. "I guess we can only keep them partly satisfied. They have enormous appetites for women. I don't really mind. I can get my rest when they're with those other women."

"I can't believe I'm saying these things to you," she added. "You're just a kid."

"I wasn't a kid last night," I said, and then hinted toward seeing if we could do it again.

"You little devil.... Let's just leave it at this one time," she said sternly but politely. I changed the subject right away. She was so nice to me I wasn't going to do anything to upset her. She never raised the subject again and never let me touch her again. However, when I was with the men, I would refer to the experience as a way of showing them that I was a man just like them. Of course, I was serious, but I think they just found it cute.

Looking back on it today, I still think she was correct in her reasons for having intercourse with me. When you could die any minute, you took what you could out of life and made the most of it. That woman taught me a lot and helped me grow up before my time. I will never forget her. She was a special person.

Jankiel and his friends were also special to me. I can still vividly recall their tough, battle-hardened faces. They were fiercely dedicated to their cause and that dedication kept them going. They worked secretly, trusting only those they knew were as committed. In secret meetings, the details of uprising attacks were worked out.

Fighting Back

On April 18, I had come into the ghetto to deliver special treats for Passover, which would begin the following evening, to my smuggling friends. That day, the ghetto received reports the Germans were congregating in massive numbers. In response, we reinforced our lookout posts that had been set up throughout the area. We confirmed the mobilization and readied ourselves for an attack. The Germans were unaware of how prepared we were.

I was staying with Jankiel's gang that anxious night. With all the activity around the ghetto walls, I wasn't going anywhere. Early the next morning, the Germans marched in. We were all asleep when we heard a knock at the door.

"Wake up, wake up!" a man yelled as loud as he could. "The swine are marching into the ghetto. Hurry, hurry to the hiding place." We scrambled to 51 Miła Street, the third house from the corner of Miła and Lubeckiego streets.

When we got there, Jankiel told the two women and me that we'd be staying at the hiding place without them. He said they were going to fight, that we'd probably never see them again. They hugged us goodbye, reached for their guns and ran off to do battle. I wanted to go with them, but they wouldn't let me — they literally shoved me into the hiding place.

Because of the first *Aktion*, I had experience with hidden attics and secret rooms. But this place was different; I had no idea a place like this bunker could even exist. It was such a well-planned space. There were three large rooms, in which about a hundred people could fit. There were even some bunk beds, a water supply (a twenty-foot-deep well) and some food to be shared by everyone. Within five minutes, the bunker was filled with people and the trap door leading to it was shut. One pleasant surprise was that I saw my friend Sewek had also been led into the room. We hadn't seen each other in a long time, so we were happy to meet up again — even if it was under such stressful circumstances.

We could hear the German army march into the ghetto. Everyone stayed totally quiet. After an hour or so, we heard sounds of battle, but we weren't sure what was going on. I wished I was out with the men to see it with my own eyes.

We later found out that the Germans entered the ghetto in two columns. Jewish combat forces were settled high up in buildings in a few different locations. The Jewish fighters had created a system allowing them to move from rooftop to rooftop, thereby avoiding the danger of the streets.

One clash took place on Nalewki Street, where bombs and hand grenades sent the Germans scrambling in shock and retreat. There was another battle at Zamenhofa and Gęsia streets, which was the site of the main German command post for the operation. On the afternoon of the second day, the fighting continued with a third confrontation at the brush factory. In all cases — even when the Germans regrouped and re-entered more prepared — the Jewish fighters had the advantage of cover, while the Germans were exposed. The first day saw the clearest Jewish victory — with only one dead fighter from the ŻOB, while the Germans had at least one death and many injured.

A few Jewish fighters showed up in our bunker, some looking like professional soldiers because they had grabbed automatic weapons, ammunition and helmets from Germans. It truly was a time to rejoice. There was a wonderful feeling of empowerment for all of us to savour.

So many courageous young people were taking part in the uprising — women as well as men. One of the people who dropped into our hideout was a woman who seemed particularly stoic. She was proudly wearing a German helmet.

I asked her where she got it. "This is a souvenir of a stinking Nazi I killed," she said. "I grabbed his gun and his helmet." I asked her if I could kiss her on her cheek for her bravery. Laughing, she granted me permission. I grasped her hand and told her I hoped she would survive the war and save that helmet to show her grandchildren one day.

I could see the tears forming in her eyes. "I don't think so," she said. "I don't think I will ever see that day. I'm ready to die any time, at any moment, and I'm happy that I was able to be a part of this movement to take revenge on the Nazis."

I knew the fighters were preparing for another attack by the Nazis when they returned the next day, so I wished her well and told her to come back in one piece. She never returned. When I heard the news, it felt like being stabbed in the chest with a knife. She was one of five young fighters who died while inflicting heavy casualties on a German command post. To me, that woman represented the essence of our movement. She was a brave young person who died with honour and dignity.

She and everyone else knew that our early success may have startled the Germans, but it wasn't going to deter them. The Nazis were going to do whatever it took to clear the ghetto, no matter how many men and weapons it required. Our side, meanwhile, only had so much weaponry — much of it of limited use. How good is a revolver when your enemy has a howitzer?

Over those few days, the ghetto transformed into an ugly war zone. The Germans became particularly vicious. Pregnant women were tortured, and mothers had their babies snatched from their arms and had to watch as soldiers saved bullets by bashing the children's heads against the wall. The tide was starting to seriously turn against us. We were dying by the hundreds, but at least many of those victims left this earth proud of their ability to resist.

Initially, the Germans believed we only had a few bunkers hidden in the ghetto. But as the operation continued, they realized that the ghetto was full of them. The Germans used special tactics such as listening devices and police dogs to find our hiding places. These tactics were only modestly effective, because we came up with our own tactics, such as chemicals to hide our scent from the dogs, along with being as quiet as possible. The most effective method used by the Germans to discover the hidden bunkers was Jewish informers — and that is how my hideout was uncovered on April 21.

We heard voices outside and knew the Germans were getting closer. Among the roughly one hundred of us down there, a baby was crying and his mother could not get him to be quiet; the man in charge of the bunker grabbed the infant from his mother's arms and choked him to death with a cushion. It was cruel, but it had to be done. There were other lives in jeopardy because of the crying. When the mother realized her baby was dead, she started to cry, so they knocked her out with a blow to the face before she became too loud.

A short while later, we heard footsteps above us. All of a sudden, we heard our trap door being ripped away. The Germans began to shout: "Raus, raus, Juden!" (Out, out, Jews!) They said we had five minutes to come out or they would throw grenades and shoot flame-throwers inside and we would all "die by being burned to a crisp."

We knew that was not an empty threat. To combat our hidden attics and bunkers, the Germans were determined to destroy every building in the ghetto. This, they thought, would assure the surrender or instant death of every Jewish inhabitant.

The Germans set about turning the ghetto into an inferno, unleashing the force of heavy artillery, including flame-throwers. Many people were burned alive. Others jumped from windows to their deaths. Being underground, we had no windows to jump from, or most of us would have leaped.

Rather than coming in after us, the Germans used the threat of fire to flush us out. I think they stayed back because they feared we had guns or that the bunker was booby-trapped with explosives. But we had neither. All our fighters were fighting. We were just hiding, so it wasn't surprising that moments after the German order, most of the people in the bunker rushed out in a panic with their hands up in the air. People were shaking with fear. Women and children were crying and screaming.

Many were disillusioned. "Where are all the fighters? Where are our heroes?" I could hear one person yell.

I didn't move. I was among the few who were using the full five minutes to choose their fate. Each person remaining in that bunker had a difficult decision to make — surrender or burn to death right there.

All of us in that small group decided to stay. I was sitting next to a woman named Frieda. She had two teenage daughters with her and told me she preferred to die there.

"What the hell. I'm going to die with the kids on the outside, so why not die right here instantly? Are you staying Jankiel?" she asked.

I had made up my mind to stay with them. I was a small boy and I knew the Germans would dispose of me — probably on the spot with a bullet to the head. I figured staying put would be a faster and more dignified death.

They then gave us one more warning — that we had two minutes to come out. At that point, my friend Sewek tried to convince me that Frieda was wrong. He said that staying in the bunker meant certain death, but on the outside — no matter how slim — at least there was a chance at survival.

"Jankiel," he said, "listen to me. On the outside we can run away while being led to the trains. If you stay here, you'll be dead within half an hour. As bad as it is, give life a chance."

He reminded me it would only be a matter of two minutes before we would be burned to death. That sent shivers down my spine. In the end, I couldn't stomach the thought of dying that way. I kissed Frieda and her daughters goodbye and made my way out of the bunker with Sewek.

Luck was on our side because no one else came with us and it had been a couple of minutes since the initial wave of people had emerged. We approached the exit and poked our heads out to see if any Germans were around. For their safety, in case any of us had weapons, they weren't right on top of the shelter. They were just outside the building, busily "processing" (searching for any valuables) the people who had already climbed out of our bunker. The Nazis were yelling at them: "If you do not give us everything you have, you will be shot on the spot. You won't ever see the labour camps."

The plunderers' preoccupying greed gave me the precious seconds I needed to get away. Barefooted to keep us as quiet as possible, I climbed out behind Sewek. I stepped on a rusty nail as we got out and my foot started to bleed profusely.

I did not even bother to look at my injury — or any of what was happening around me. All I wanted to do was run. It was as though a higher power compelled me to just run. I knew there was a good chance that I would be spotted and shot in the back of the head. I also knew that would have been a fast and painless end — better than being sent to Treblinka or burned to death in that bunker.

As Sewek joined the group being readied for Treblinka, I dashed across the street and was wildly lucky to be undetected. I was in the remains of a house that had just burned down. Among the mud and debris, I saw two dead bodies — a man and a woman. They had both been shot in the head. I lay down next to them in the mud as if I too had been shot dead.

I shivered from the cold dampness. It was a creepy situation; it seemed as if the dead bodies were staring at me. Nonetheless, I wasn't going anywhere until I heard the Germans march off. I tore a piece off my shirt, wrapped it around my foot wound, and stayed quietly still.

With my eyes tightly closed most of the time, I listened intently trying to determine what was happening. I could hear light trucks followed by heavier tanks being brought into the ghetto. Then I could hear artillery shells exploding. The houses of our resistance fighters were being decimated; our men and women were severely outmatched.

I was terrified as I curled up in that mud. *What am I doing here? If I survive till dark, where am I going to go?* I cried to myself. I wasn't really talking to myself, but to my dead parents. I was looking for their help to get me out of this horrible situation, lying next to two dead bodies and surrounded by a chaotic inferno. If hell is how the Christians describe it, it must be a much more pleasant place than where I was.

About thirty minutes later, I thought I could hear the Germans marching off into the distance. It was finally safe to open my eyes. Then I got up — wet, cold and covered in mud.

I took a closer look at the two bodies to see if I knew them. I think they were both in their twenties, but it was hard to tell for sure because their faces were so bloodied and disfigured. They must have been two fighters shot during battle. I did not know who they were but I was sure they had fought valiantly for our cause.

I ran to a nearby house that wasn't as damaged and figured I could hide in it until dark. I did not know what would happen next. Would I end up just like the corpses I had just hidden among — shot to death in such a godforsaken inferno? I tried to block those thoughts. I focused on making it until nightfall, when I would go back to our original bunker to see if anyone else was there. I thought maybe by some miracle someone else had survived.

But no matter how hard I tried, I could not ignore the reality of the situation. I started to cry profusely; I had witnessed so much tragedy and sorrow in just a few short hours. I began to regret being alone; maybe I should have just died with all the others. I started thinking more about what might have happened to all those people in our hiding place. Were they really burned to death? Then I thought about the remains of my body had I stayed there. It would just be a charred mess, and there would be no one to bury me. I cried for a few more minutes, but then I regained my composure, and made my move toward our hideout. I was too anxious to wait until dark.

I looked both ways for Germans and made a run for it. When I saw a soldier on the other side of the street, I detoured into 11 Wołyńska Street, a burned-out apartment building that I could hide in. At the rear of the building, I found a laundry tub. I pulled it toward me such that I could peer out above it but would be hidden from view when I ducked. I felt reasonably safe in this empty building. Its residents must have jumped to their deaths or surrendered.

Lying there, I could do nothing but think about my live-or-die dilemma, and death was winning. I wondered what I had really accomplished. Had I run away from my friends just so I could die alone a few hours later? At least in the bunker I knew the people and had the comfort of dying collectively.

I also started to think again about what would become of my body after death. I would be a hearty meal for the German shepherd dogs or the ghetto's sizable rat population. My mind was racing, and between the intense heat and unmanageable anxiety, my heart felt like an overworked motor about to explode. I was also dying of thirst. It was so hot in that freshly burned building that I had to take all my clothes off.

A few minutes after I arrived, I heard German voices getting closer and closer. Soon they were so near I could hear exactly what they were saying and could see everything they did. I saw a few of them urinate no more than twenty feet from me. I was angry at myself for having left the safety of my spot beside those two dead bodies.

I was terrified but stayed silent and was fortunate to be undetected. A few minutes later, I heard the sound of dishes and saw a big red pot with steam coming out of it. It was time for their lunch, a break from Jew hunting.

After a while, they finished their meal and left. I stuck my head out for fresh air as relief from the unbearable heat. I was desperate for some water but didn't want to risk walking out of that building. There may still have been a guard or two there, so I waited until dark.

As I lay there all afternoon, I continued to hear lots of shooting, explosions and artillery fire. I was hoping that the Germans were at least suffering a few casualties in those battles.

Darkness finally neared, so I got dressed into my clothes, looked carefully to see if anyone was nearby, and left the building. I knew the Germans departed for the night; it was to their advantage to work in daylight when they could uncover hiding places and be better prepared for hit-and-run fighters.

With some high-rises still burning, I headed toward our hideout — the place I had fled at the start of the day. Even though it was just a short walk away, it was a painful one. My foot was severely cut, and the pavement was still hot from all the fire.

I could not believe the scene. The first thing I noticed was the unmistakable stench of death. Burned flesh has a horrendously powerful odour. My disgust was matched by the sight of burned bodies. All that was left of my friends who chose not to come out was a jumble of bone fragments — barely recognizable body parts. The Germans hadn't just threatened us. They really did torch the place by throwing several grenades in and then lighting the building on fire. It was still smouldering.

I sat down and began to cry hysterically. I cried for myself and for the friends I had left in the bunker. I thought about Frieda and her two daughters, who tried to convince me to stay behind with them — how they were now just burned remains. It made me sick to my stomach. I wanted to vomit, but that was impossible because I had no food in my stomach.

I said a prayer for them, even though I no longer believed in the existence of the Almighty anymore. If there really were a God, how could he let all this happen? All these little children had been slaughtered, and they never even had a chance to sin — never even knew what the word meant. Where was God for them? Why had he not struck all the Nazis dead? I was bitter and hurt. And my morbid thoughts continued: when and how was I going to die?

In the midst of my crying, I felt a tap on my shoulder and leaped with fear. Still wrapped up with all those thoughts of my burned friends, I thought it was a ghost. When I turned around, I saw my fighter friends, Szlojme, Aaron, Jacob and Jankiel. They could not believe their eyes when they saw me. We embraced with joy.

"How did you get here?" they asked. "How is it that you're alive and all the others are dead?" I explained what had happened, including the two bodies I hid next to. Then I asked them the same question, and they said they had hid in the sewers while all the destruction was occurring. Realizing how lucky we were to cross paths again, they promised to take me with them wherever they went and to not let me out of their sight. This gave me a feeling of much-needed security.

We said Kaddish for the people from our bunker — the closest we could come to giving them a decent burial. I took the men to where the two fighters had died, and they searched them for identification. They were a married couple. Aaron knew the man. As tough a man as Aaron was, he seemed extremely shaken by the discovery.

My friends dug a small grave. We said a prayer as we put the couple's remains in the ground and then covered the hole with dirt. I wonder if their bones are still buried there today.

As we prepared to move on, a part of me envied the charred remains of those fighters. Their ordeal was over while I was still waiting for my resolution. I couldn't stop thinking about death. Would I be shot? Would I be sent away? Most twelve-year-olds were probably concerned with tomorrow's test in school, while I was contemplating what form my certain death would take.

With the bodies buried, my friends took me on what they called a mission. When I asked what it was, they told me I would find out soon enough.

Within an hour, we had tracked down the hiding place of a Jewish man named Schmuel. Earlier that day, he had been seen showing bunker locations to the Germans. My friends confronted this man, who was about their age. They yelled at him, calling him a "rotten traitor" for giving away the locations of seven Jewish hiding places, including the one I was in. In return for his cowardly act, the Germans gave him some food and the promise that his life would be spared. It was well known that the Germans killed all their Jewish informers as soon as they were no longer of use to them, but it didn't seem to deter some people like Schmuel.

My friends told the man he had betrayed them unforgivably. Each pulled out his pistol and fired two shots into the traitor. When they were sure he was dead, they pulled his fancy boots off and threw his body into a cellar, hoping the Germans would find the corpse and get the message. Now that I knew he was the one who had given my hiding place away to the Germans, I wished the men had given me a pistol to help kill him.

My friends told me that the next morning Schmuel was to meet the Germans to reveal more hiding places for more food. We saved a few lives by killing him before he could do more damage. They took out a bottle of booze, and we each had a swig. We left feeling relieved and satisfied with the execution.

It was now well into the evening and time to return to their hiding place — a sewer canal at the corner of Lubeckiego and Miła. It was a disgusting scene — the sewage system was putrid and full of huge rats, which we had to ward off.

As soon as we arrived, we had something to eat — my first meal of the day. The men had kept some food in steel containers for protection against the rats. Our mealtime discussion focused on what had happened in the previous few hours of battle.

"Yes, we killed plenty of those bastards," said Jankiel, "but not as many as we would have liked. They brought in heavy artillery, tanks and eventually even planes to bomb each and every house on every street in the ghetto. That's why you saw it all ablaze," he told me.

Now that I had a chance to reflect, I realized how lucky I was — to leave with Sewek, get by undetected, safely hide through the day and then be found by my friends. Had they not seen me, I don't know what I would have done. My legs were paralyzed with fear just thinking about it.

When I went to sleep on my wet and foul-smelling mattress, my thoughts turned to my brother Eli. Not only was I worried about him, but I realized he would be nervously wondering if I was alive or not. I really wanted to get back out and see him again as soon as possible.

It was clear the Jewish resistance was not going to last much longer. Our numbers were dwindling, ammunition was running out, the ghetto was burning to ashes and food was scarce. But we didn't feel defeated. We knew from the start that we were no match for the Germans, but dying in battle gave some meaning to our inevitable death. They could kill us but they could never take our accomplishments away from the history books.

We realized, however, that it was best at that point to get out of there and try to survive outside the ghetto. We were convinced it would only be a matter of hours before the Germans obliterated us and the rest of the ghetto. The sewers were our only haven, as the Germans weren't wise to them yet, but that wouldn't last long either.

Although the uprising would last for another three weeks of fighting, the final outcome was clear. The next day — my twelfth birthday — we formulated our plans for getting out.

Never Safe

We decided our best chance to escape the ghetto was through the sewers. These wound all the way through Warsaw, and we thought there was probably a route that would take us to an access cover that exited onto the "Aryan" side. Jankiel said it was up to Aaron and me to determine the route.

We figured it was too risky to go during the day, so we arranged to conduct our search after dark. Our plan was to spend the night trying to find a path, return to our "base" and then leave permanently with the others the following night.

Aaron and I set out late in the evening, taking two large candles with us, along with a flashlight to be used sparingly. Before leaving, we made a kind of glue out of flour and water, and cut some refuse paper into small pieces. We used these to create numbered stickers that could be put on the sewer walls to mark where we'd been so we wouldn't get lost and to provide us with a route to follow for the final departure.

The sewers were about three or four feet high. That wasn't much of a problem for me because I was so small — which was why I was chosen for the assignment. But it was a different story for Aaron. Even though he was the youngest and shortest of the four men, he was still close to six feet tall, so his back became extremely sore as the journey progressed. We were also wading in smelly raw sewage, with rats scurrying all around us. It was a disgusting breeding ground for disease.

To take our minds off our surroundings, we talked about all the experiences each of us had been through and friends of ours who had fought in the ghetto battles. Zlata was a large part of that conversation. Aaron asked me if I knew what happened to her. I told him she was taken away along with the many others in our bunker who had surrendered. I then paused for a moment and added that perhaps she had survived because she was a strong and healthy twenty-eight-year-old — the Germans may have put her to work instead of sending her to the gas chambers. It was a night to be upbeat, as we were hoping to escape, and I didn't want to fill it with negative thoughts. Realistically, however, we both knew that Zlata and all the others shipped off were probably dead by now.

After crawling for about three hours, we finally reached a spot we were quite certain led to a street on the "Aryan" side. There were about twenty steps to climb before reaching the access cover. I marked the location of that ladder with the three largest stickers, labelled with the words "Aryan Side." We could now return to the others, feeling good that we had accomplished our mission. By following our own markings, we made it back in about an hour.

When we returned, we told the other men that the only obstacle was removing the heavy access cover. Jankiel said he'd need some time to acquire some tools to pry the plate open. Perhaps because of that, or for some other reason unknown to me, he decided that we'd leave forty-eight hours later instead of the next night. The minor delay didn't bother us. We were optimistic about our chances and looking forward to the journey.

After getting a little rest in the morning, we started the afternoon of our first waiting day by getting organized to leave. Then, late that afternoon, we heard screaming in the distance — and the voices were getting closer. Soon, there was a funny smell in the air.

Just a few blocks away, a Jewish hideout linked to the sewers had been discovered. After saturating the location with gas, and seeing none in the group of maybe two hundred people there flee, the Germans must have become suspicious, entered the building and discovered a connection to the underground system. They reacted by pumping massive amounts of poison gas into the sewer.

As quickly as we could, we attempted to get away through the sewers where we were hiding from the other fleeing Jews and the Nazis. Unfortunately, our labelled route out of the ghetto would have taken us toward the fugitives before looping around to the "Aryan" side. All our stickers were now useless. We were just scrambling to stay ahead of the oncoming men, women and children.

Within ten or fifteen minutes, we spotted a ladder going up to a street. Arriving there a couple of minutes in advance of the first fleeing Jews, I ran up the metal steps, squeezing beside my friends so each of us could get as close as possible to the access lid. We took turns breathing fresh air through its tiny holes. When all the others made it to our spot, they wanted to climb up and breathe too, but there was barely enough air and space for my friends and me. As the terrified Jews struggled to climb the ladder, we instinctively kicked them down to the ground. It was selfish but when you're fighting for survival you just react and do whatever is required.

With the concentration of gas increasing, it didn't take long for the people under us to start losing consciousness. Moments later we were beginning to feel overcome ourselves. We could not wait any longer, so we pushed and pushed and managed to flip open the cover. We jumped out and ran across the street as fast as we could. We expected to be shot in the process, but to our amazement there were no Germans around.

After we crossed the road, my friends said to follow them to one or two hideouts nearby. They weren't sure whether these were still intact, but we had no choice but to find out. We went to one just down the street and were relieved that despite the German attacks, a group of people they knew remained in hiding there. And we were even luckier with some remarkable timing. The group there of about twenty-five people was getting ready to leave the ghetto that night, having arranged for two Poles who worked in the sewers to lead them out. Each night, after the Germans left the ghetto for the day, these two men would take a group of Jews to the other side.

Late that night, all of us waited at a designated spot a few blocks away, hoping for the sewer workers to show up. A short while later, a tall, thin Polish man arrived. Having already travelled through the sewer to get to us, he looked like a big banana in his yellow rubber boots and coveralls.

"Let's go," he said. "Whoever is ready, we're going now. Make sure you have your payments ready."

This was news to me — and sent a shiver down my spine. I should have known profit was the only reason they would help Jews. The fee was five thousand złotys, or an equivalent amount in gold or jewellery. All I had was my little bag filled with candles from our sticker-making trip. I think he assumed the sack was filled with valuables, and I didn't say or do anything that would make him think otherwise. I gripped it as if it were filled with jewels.

As we departed, I went to the front of the line, close behind the sewer man. He must not have had his dinner yet, as he pulled a loaf of bread and a large piece of sausage from his bag. I couldn't help but stare at his food. I was so hungry I would have given my right arm for some of it. When he saw me staring, he cut a piece of bread and sausage for me. "Here," he yelled — and tossed the food to me. I gobbled it down within seconds. It tasted delicious and gave me energy for the trip ahead.

The arrangement was that we would pay him when he got us to the other side. That was fair, because if we had paid before the trip he could have just taken the money and turned us over to the Germans. We set off, and I remained right behind the man's rubber pants. He was familiar with the sewers and moved quickly. The few of us at the front could keep up, but most of the group had difficulty. We had to stop several times and wait for them to catch up.

About thirty minutes later, we arrived at the ladder that led outside the ghetto. Just before it was my turn to climb out, the sewer worker demanded payment from me. Rather than give him my bag, I told him that my father was among those at the back of the group, and he would pay for me when he caught up to us. The man gave me a strange look but said that was okay as long as I stayed near him until my father showed up. The man then began collecting payment from the others as they arrived. As soon as they paid him, they'd go up the ladder.

A few minutes later, when he had six to eight people to deal with, he seemed to forget about me, so I went up the stairs with those who had just paid. After climbing about twenty steps, we were at street level, where another Polish man was waiting to pull us out. It was well after curfew, so he was risking his life to be there. But the risk was minimized by having chosen a quiet, dead-end street unlikely to be patrolled.

The Jews just stood on the street quietly, waiting for all the others to arrive, when they would all be led off by the workers. I decided to run for my life. I couldn't take the chance that the worker would see me again and demand payment. It was the last I saw of any of those people — including my four friends.

I ran for a few blocks until I came to a large apartment building that looked inviting. I quietly entered the lobby and noticed that there was a washroom. It had about twelve toilet stalls, along with a hose that delivered running water. I smelled like the sewer, so I thoroughly washed myself and tried to clean my clothes. I hid in a stall until morning to ensure I would not be caught after curfew. Waiting also gave my clothes a little time to dry.

As I sat there, all I could think about was seeing my brother Eli again. Just the thought of him made me happy and full of hope, which is something I really needed considering the three days of hell I had just been through.

I left the building a few hours later when the sun rose and jumped on the tail of a streetcar going to Praga. I arrived at Eli's building and entered the converted stable he was staying in. But he wasn't there. I looked all over the place, and he was nowhere to be found.

I went to visit the woman who owned the stable to see if she knew where he was. She turned pale and said she had bad news for me. She said that a suspicious neighbour had called the police the day before to say a Jewish boy was hiding on her street. When the authorities came, she said, they approached her demanding to know the truth. She told them she had no idea what they were talking about but that if a Jew was staying on her property it was without her knowledge, and she agreed he should be caught.

Apparently, Eli had seen them coming. While they were talking to the owner, he had fled to the cellar of another house. Someone who saw him flee informed the police.

I was told they approached the cellar with their guns drawn — as though Eli were some kind of dangerous gangster. All they found was a frightened little boy curled up in a corner crying. The men pulled my little brother out by his long blond hair and started beating him with their sticks. I was told they savagely pounded him, even though he offered no resistance. All he did was repeatedly call out my name. "Janek, Janek, help me. Where are you? Help me."

I don't know what they ended up doing with him — whether they shot him, tortured him or sent him away to a death camp. All I know is that he was never heard from again. I tried to identify the person who had called the police but could not learn anything more than that it was a woman resident of that street. Had I found her, I was enraged enough to get a gun and shoot the heartless scum. I would have gladly traded my life to take revenge on the person responsible.

It was frustrating to be told that all the neighbours had gathered to watch the incident. How could the people who witnessed the episode not feel sorry for the little boy and do something to help? These people who watched had children of their own, and the two policemen may have had children as well. How could they be so cruel? At least the woman who owned the building had the decency to tell me what had happened and did not turn me in, even though by this time she knew for certain I was Jewish.

The whole time I was in the ghetto, I was more worried about myself than Eli. After all, he was on the outside in a protected location. When we had found that place, I thought it would be our haven. I really believed it would give him a good chance of surviving the war — an opportunity to grow up and become a special young man. The barbarity of the Germans and the Poles meant that he never got the chance. I again learned the lesson that in Warsaw there was no such thing as safety for a Jew.

All Eli and I had really had in life was each other. I hate to imagine how he must have felt when he called out for me — the only person on this cruel earth who could help him — only to be left on his own, sentenced to a painful death. I felt sick to my stomach. The war was making me witness the worst of humanity; there was no end to the ruthlessness.

Eli lost his life over the tiny reward — a bit of money or three kilos of sugar — received by that despicable neighbour.

At first, I felt guilty, thinking that had I not been involved in the uprising in the ghetto perhaps I could have saved my brother. On the other hand, I realized that I too would have been taken away — though at least we would have died together.

Eli and I were all that was left of what was once a large family. We understood that as long as we had each other, we still had a sense of family, and with it, a shred of normality in life. So many times when I wanted to die, it was the thought of Eli that kept me going. Losing him was the toughest blow of all.

To add to the torment, it happened just after my birthday. What a present — nothing but tragedy and sorrow. Tears kept filling my eyes. I wondered how much more I could take. I was now truly alone. I felt close to taking my own life, but I found the motivation to survive.

I decided that keeping the family name alive and telling the world what the Nazis had done to Eli and my family was enough incentive to keep living.

And I did have a glimmer of hope. At least I was outside the ghetto. There was no time to mourn. I had to focus on surviving. I realized I had to flee that place immediately because the same person who gave my brother away could call the police and have me taken away as well.

I left for Saska Kępa, which was a different neighbourhood a few miles away where my friends Paweł, Zenek and Zbyszek operated. With a heavy heart, I went back to what I knew best. I knocked on some doors in a rich neighbourhood and started begging; I got some bread and a little meat. I had no appetite but knew my stomach needed some food in it.

The first few nights after learning Eli had died were emotionally devastating. It was early springtime, warm enough that I could sleep in the park or other outdoor sites. I would cry myself to sleep, thinking constantly about how much I missed my brother. I still don't know how I managed to stay sane.

A Place to Sleep, a Place to Stay Dry

I slowly got myself into the rhythm of survival again. I obtained a new cross to wear around my neck and resumed my tried-and-true begging-and-singing method.

One warm night I chose to sleep in the local amusement park that had closed for the night. I found a swinging ride with two or three compartments, each designed to hold two people. It seemed to be a safe, quiet and relatively comfortable place to spend the night.

About half an hour after lying down, I heard footsteps approaching the ride. I had to hide. I was small enough to be totally concealed after climbing under the two-person seat in my compartment. As the voices neared, I could hear that it was a man and a woman, both speaking German. From what I heard them say, it seemed they worked together in an office and were on a date. Without lifting my head, I stayed motionless, waiting for them to finish their discussion and leave. But they weren't going anywhere. He was trying to convince her to have sex with him there in the swing. She didn't want to but eventually gave in, and they entered the compartment where I was hiding.

They proceeded to have sex, inches above my head. I was lying flat on my back, getting sick to my stomach as the swing went up and down repeatedly. Soon after they finished the act they left, and I fell asleep — completely exhausted. I was lucky to get by undetected and never went back there.

As I had learned with Eli, the heavily forested park was usually the most convenient and hassle-free location for sleeping, but I encountered a few scary moments there too.

The Germans were serious about the city's 9:00 p.m. curfew. There were some people who tried to stay out later, but they were foolish. Jeep patrols drove around all night and would often shoot first and ask questions later when they saw people on the streets. It didn't matter if it was two lovebirds or a vagrant child. Many Poles were killed this way.

One night I shared an area of the park with a Polish couple who had realized it was too late to get home safely after their dinner date and evening stroll. They shared a bottle of vodka and spent the night having sex in the bushes.

I didn't dare sleep that night. Had they come near me to urinate, for example, I could have been discovered and reported. Instead of sleeping, I entertained myself by listening to them all night long. I could hear them talk dirty when they had sex and was able to add to my vocabulary what felt like every Polish profanity ever uttered.

The park was more than just a place to sleep. On the nights when it was cold so no one else was around — after midnight but well before dawn, when it was darkest — I would slip into the river and wash myself. Some days I emerged from the river as red as a tomato because the water was so cold, but I felt healthy and strong and didn't let it bother me. I needed that mental toughness. I couldn't allow the cold to affect me because I simply could not afford to get sick. Illness was a death notice. Whenever I felt unwell, I had to convince myself that I was fine and just kept going, forcing myself to recover quickly.

On especially damp and chilly days, I needed creative ways to keep warm. The churches were an excellent solution. They always kept their doors open for fine young Catholics. I would enter the church, kneel down and go through the motions of praying. I learned all the Catholic prayers and even went to church services on Sundays.

The priests liked it when I was there, relishing the chance to talk with such a religious young person.

One time a priest asked where my parents were. I told him my mother was dead and my father was bitter about losing her, so he stopped believing in God. This got the priest interested in my life, and he tried hard to become my friend. He continued to ask so many questions about my family that I stopped going to his church. After that, I rotated churches because I did not want to let any priest get to know me too well and start asking personal questions that could reveal my identity.

When I tried a church run by a man called Father Jan, I quickly realized he was different than the other priests. He was younger and seemed more in tune with regular people. He was friendly but gave me my space and didn't pressure me with personal questions.

"Have you come here to pray because you are so religious?" he asked after letting me kneel alone for most of my first visit. "Or is it just that this is a place where you can stay warm and dry?"

I told him I came for both reasons. I said that I was a firm believer in Jesus and that I enjoyed praying, but a life on the streets meant I also needed a place to stay dry.

"Is it all right to do so, Father?" I asked. "Is it all right to come in here?"

"My son, come in as many times as you like. It is perfectly all right, perfectly all right."

Had he known I was Jewish, I am not sure he would have felt the same way. I was not about to take that chance.

I felt more comfortable there than at any of the other churches and abandoned my own rule of not repeatedly going to one location. I made his church a regular part of my routine. I even went to Father Jan for confession on several occasions.

I got to know Father Jan. Over time, he did start to ask more probing questions, but he never went too far. I told him that I lived with an aunt, that my parents had died in a traffic accident two years previously. I described having to beg on the streets to help her pay the bills. When he asked why my aunt never went to church, I told him she was an atheist who refused to go but that I was praying she would have a revelation some day and change her ways. With all the lies I was telling, I suppose it was a good thing we had those confession sessions.

Father Jan seemed to be a good person. Perhaps he had suspicions about whether my story was true, but he never said anything that would make me feel threatened.

It was difficult living a lie all the time because I had to keep my guard up at all times. I had to think carefully before I said anything. All it took to be turned in was for one wrong word to slip out. It was hard to stay so alert all the time.

There were a few precious moments when I felt like I could partially escape my situation. One of those moments was when, once a week or so, I would treat myself to a show. I would bribe the doorman with ten cigarettes to let me in to the theatre.

I would get a snack and settle into a chair in the empty rows at the front of the theatre. It was two hours of feeling like any other theatregoer. When the lights came on, it was back to reality. Everyone else had a home to return to, while I had to run out of there and search for shelter for the night, knowing that I could be caught any time. It was a difficult transition — from the joy of watching the play to the stress of seeking refuge.

One rainy night I was looking for somewhere to sleep and ended up at 5 Radziłowska Street, a four- or five-storey apartment building. Next to its back door was a shed containing eight large garbage cans. I entered the shed and arranged the containers so that I could lie down behind them without being seen if someone came in to throw out their trash. I stole a straw mat from the doorway of one of the apartments, laid it on the cement as a mattress and used a large potato bag as a blanket. I went to sleep very late because I was afraid I might snore and be discovered by a resident.

Early the next morning, I was awoken by rustling noises above me. I lay there quietly, listening intently but unsure exactly what was going on. I was gripped with fear. The cans were being moved into their original position, and within a few moments I was exposed and vulnerable. I curled myself up in a ball.

A tall woman around forty years old towered over me.

"My God!" she shrieked, thinking she had stumbled across a dead body. Reluctantly, I looked up, and she realized I was alive.

"Who are you? What are you doing here? Get up, little boy! This is no place for sleeping!" she snapped.

We stared at each other for a moment or two, and I began to spin another tale to try to get myself safely out of there.

I told her I was from a farm outside Warsaw and just wanted to spend a day in the big city. I said I had hitchhiked into town and spent the day touring around. I explained that I needed a place to sleep for the night. I had no money for a room, so this spot looked as good as any.

"But now that it's morning, I'll head back," I said. "Sorry if I've caused you any inconvenience."

This woman looked unimpressed. "You're not fooling me," she said, staring me straight in the eye. "You're a Jewish boy in hiding, aren't you? Don't be afraid. Tell me the truth. I won't give you away."

I told her again that I was a gentile boy. "Look at my cross," I said. "I can recite some prayers for you. Believe me, I'm telling you the truth. I'm not a Jew."

But she wouldn't let the issue rest.

"You'd better be honest with me," she said. "Are you really a Jewish boy? If you'll just tell me the truth, I'll let you sleep there as long as you want. I don't care. I won't tell anybody. But I demand that you tell me the truth."

I still wouldn't change my story, so she finally dropped the issue and changed the subject.

"All right," she said, "whatever your story is, you must be hungry.

·

Why don't you come to my apartment for a bite to eat?"

My head told me it was a trap. Maybe I should just make a run for it? But I was hungry and took the risk, following her into the building.

She had a modest apartment — a bathroom and one main room, which had space for not much more than a couple of beds, a few kitchen appliances and a table.

The woman offered me a cup of hot chocolate. She also gave me some bread and butter.

"I bet you didn't have much to eat yesterday," she said. I insisted that was not true, but it was difficult to hide how anxious I was to eat.

I changed the subject, asking if she lived there alone. She said she had two teenage daughters, but now that summer holidays had begun they were both away at their grandmother's farm. They would be back in ten days, she said.

I asked if her husband was with the girls. My question seemed to upset her, but she reluctantly told me they had been separated for three years. She felt sorry for her daughters, growing up without a father. "Otherwise," she said, "I don't miss him at all. He's not really worth talking about. He was abusive and an alcoholic."

Then she paused for a moment before she went too far.

"I don't know why I'm telling you all this. I have just found you among garbage cans and here I am telling you my most personal details — and you're what — maybe twelve years old." I told her she had guessed my age exactly.

As our conversation went on, it became clear to me that she was a good person. She had been so honest with me I finally decided to trust her and reciprocate. I was still worried that I was making a big mistake, but I admitted that I was a Jewish boy, who had lost his whole family — the sole survivor among perhaps a hundred relatives. I was crying as I told her about my parents' deaths in the ghetto, how Brenda and Menashe were taken away to the camps, and how I had just lost Eli. I described how I lived on the streets — surviving day-to-day but knowing I could die at any moment.

She started to cry with me and gave me an affectionate hug. It was as though she could feel my pain, as a mother would feel for a child. She kept repeating over and over what a tragedy my life was.

"This is what Hitler has brought to our country," she said. "He's ruined it for all of us, though I know we've got it a lot better than your people."

My instincts told me this woman was genuine. She had become emotional listening to me. I had strict rules about not trusting any-one, but in this case I felt compelled to make an exception. Looking into her eyes, I could tell she wasn't tricking me. It seemed she really did care for me.

We talked for a couple of hours, as I told her all the details about what had happened to me. At the end of the conversation, we ex-changed names. I told her that my real name was Jankiel, but that I had to go by Janek. Her name was Mrs. Lodzia. Her absent daughters were Irka, who was fifteen years old, and Marysia, who was thirteen.

Mrs. Lodzia was poor, making just enough to support her family in their small apartment. She was the superintendent of the building and to make ends meet she did the rich tenants' laundry and ironing.

As I was getting ready to leave, she grabbed me by the arm and said to wait a minute. She went to the bathroom and turned the water on to fill the tub. She said I was dirty and should clean myself. I was thrilled by the idea. The hot, soapy water felt luxurious; I couldn't remember the last time I had taken a real bath.

After I dried off, Mrs. Lodzia said she wanted to help me on a permanent basis. She insisted that I sleep in her home.

When, worried, I brought up that the penalty for hiding a Jew is death, she told me she didn't care. She said we'd worry about what her daughters thought when they returned in ten days.

I was stunned at her compassion, and all I could do was thank her repeatedly and gush over her kindness. If only everyone were like her. What a place the world would be. I told her what a wonderful person she was.

The plan was that I would continue with my normal activities on the streets during the day. At night, I would come "home" to Mrs. Lodzia's to sleep under the kitchen table. The table was right by the window, and because we were on the ground floor and the window opened onto an alley leading to a street, I could quickly escape if police came knocking late at night. I slept in my clothes in case that happened.

Things went really well for the next week and a half, and Mrs. Lodzia was consistently kind toward me. When her daughters came home from the farm, however, they were in for a shock. They walked in the door and there I was.

"Who is this?" they asked in unison. "Who is this boy and what is he doing here?" Their mother told them to sit down and she would explain.

"This is Janek. He is Jewish and is the last survivor of his family. I feel nothing but pity for him and I believe you should too. We should all help him."

"But you know what the posters say," Irka said. "If you harbour a Jew, the whole family will be shot."

"Yes, I know about that," her mother replied. "But does he look Jewish to you? He looks as gentile as us. And if anyone asks we'll say he's a cousin from the farm and that he's just staying for a few days. Then he'll leave and that will be that. But for now, it's important we do what we can for him, and that no one knows our secret."

Within a couple of minutes, the sisters came to fully support their mother's decision to let me stay there. I even became good friends with the girls — as though they were my older sisters and I was the brother they never had.

When Mrs. Lodzia had to go visit her mother for a few days, which happened from time to time, she left Irka in charge, which included being responsible for all the superintendent chores. With Mrs. Lodzia away, Irka and Marysia decided on one occasion to have some fun one night. After I said goodnight to them and crawled under the table, I heard some whispering and giggling. Then Irka said to me:

"How would you like to come sleep with us? You could come snuggle into this nice warm bed right between us. Why don't you go wash yourself and climb in with us? It will be much nicer than sleeping on the floor."

I told her I couldn't, that her mother would not approve. I said she was trusting us to behave while she was away and would kick me out if she found out.

"Oh Janek, don't be such a bore. Mother will never know," she said. "We give you our word we will not say anything."

I reiterated that I would love to do it but just couldn't take the chance. I argued that they might get angry with me sometime in the future and tell their mother about the incident in the heat of the moment.

They thought that was nonsense and said they'd make me change my mind. They literally held me down and undressed me — not that I was resisting too much. Then they "forced" me to climb into bed with them.

I shared the bed with the sisters for three consecutive nights. Each night I was the perfect gentleman, never touching either of them inappropriately. It felt good to sleep in a bed for the first time in ages — and it made me feel like part of the family. I thanked them for a special memory.

Something unusual seemed to occur whenever someone was at the grandmother's farm. One time, when the girls were away for a weekend, I was exposed to a different side of Mrs. Lodzia.

For a short while, she had been seeing a married man who owned a grocery store. They kept their affair quiet — never appearing together in public, and he would only come over occasionally. With the girls away, he came by unexpectedly one evening while I was in the apartment. When Mrs. Lodzia heard the knock at the door, she thought it was a tenant and told me to hide behind the curtains where her clothes were hanging.

"How are you, stranger?" I heard him ask as she opened the door. "I apologize for showing up unannounced, but I had a yearning for you and I've come with some vodka and goodies so maybe we can spend some time together."

She invited him in. I was still hidden and had to keep quiet — I couldn't even let myself fall asleep and risk snoring. Not far from me, they proceeded to have sex. I kept myself awake by focusing on their activities, just as I had done weeks earlier in the park. I could see the shadows of their movements and hear every word they spoke. It was amusing and educational stuff, but it was exhausting forcing myself to remain awake and keep still for several hours. When he finally left late in the night, I emerged from hiding.

"Well, now you know everything about me," she said, "even my private life."

Her relationship with the grocer ended soon after — the man's wife was starting to get suspicious.

Sometime after this event, I was looking for Mrs. Lodzia on a hot summer day and went searching for her in the attic, where I knew she was likely doing laundry. I ran up there and found the door locked. I knocked and told her it was me, so she invited me in.

I was shocked to see that she was naked. Almost as remarkable as the sight itself was the fact that she didn't seem to care that I was seeing her naked. She could have put her clothes on and then let me in, but I suppose she couldn't be bothered. Maybe she thought this was nothing compared to having watched her have sex.

"Janek, you see these legs," she said to me. "I hope men turn their heads at them. What do you think? Are these legs nice?" She may have been fishing for a compliment, but she deserved one. She was about five feet, ten inches tall, blond and possessed a body that did turn many heads.

"Yes, Mrs. Lodzia, they are beautiful, and you have a gorgeous figure to go with them. And I might add you have a friendly and pretty face."

I could not understand how that husband of hers could have been so stupid as to lose such a beautiful and caring woman with two delightful daughters. I told her that if I were to survive the war and grow into manhood, I would try to be lucky to find a woman as insightful, compassionate and attractive as she was.

"Janek, you flatter me. We both know that I am fast becoming an old woman," she laughed. "But I like and appreciate what you are saying. You have an old head on your shoulders. You know how to make a woman feel good, and that is a good thing, a very good thing.

"Women like to be complimented, a nice word here and there. Remember what I'm telling you. Some day you might be able to put it to good use with some lucky girl." We had these conversations many more times. I always enjoyed them.

After the ghetto and the horrible period following Eli's death, staying with Mrs. Lodzia finally gave me something to be happy about. Mrs. Lodzia was a guardian angel. She was — and remains — a major influence on my life. I can never express how lucky I am to have slept in that garbage shed the night she found me.

I met Mrs. Lodzia in mid-1943; the end of the war was still nowhere in sight. There remained many more challenges on the road to survival. Without Mrs. Lodzia, I wouldn't have had a chance.

The Cigarette Sellers

Life with Mrs. Lodzia and her daughters brought me great joy, and I was also fortunate to have some great friends who were also like family to me.

While hustling on the streets, I spent a lot of time with Zbyszek, Paweł and Zenek, the Jewish boys Eli and I had met in 1942. After Eli died, these friends tried hard to ease my pain by maintaining an upbeat attitude. They were true friends, dependable people whom I knew really cared for me. There was something special about being with others who shared my predicament.

I thought the four of us were the only boys who had escaped the ghetto and were still alive. But one day in the summer of 1943 I discovered that there were others. I was walking with Paweł when we came across a boy and girl singing under a bridge. The boy looked familiar to me. Within a moment or two, I remembered that he was from my family's neighbourhood and his name was Boluś.

He recognized me as I recognized him, and we greeted each other with warmth, but in a quiet way so as not to draw attention to ourselves.

"I didn't think there were any other survivors," he said. "I thought all the Jewish kids left were selling cigarettes in Three Crosses Square."

Three Crosses Square was right in the heart of the German quarter, the area of Warsaw reserved for the Germans. It was tough to believe that any other Jewish children could be alive, let alone interacting with German soldiers. I told Boluś I didn't believe him, adding that he shouldn't joke about such a serious matter. But he insisted he was telling the truth. He said we could meet them if we wanted. So a rendezvous was arranged for the next day at Three Crosses Square where we would be introduced to the rest of these children.

Boluś wasn't lying. There were about a dozen young Jewish boys selling cigarettes in the area. From the moment we exchanged greetings, we felt as though we had known each other all our lives. Perhaps misery loves company, but despite age and personality differences among the group we all hit it off. Joining this larger group provided a significant morale boost.

The leader of the gang was a boy named Irving — known to everyone as Bull, a strong character who was a few years older than me. Others in the group included Conky, named for his big nose, two boys named Stasiek — one was called Golec and the other Little Stasiek — and an extremely handsome young man with a great big smile named Romek.

Almost immediately, Zbyszek, Paweł, Zenek and I began selling cigarettes with these other boys at Three Crosses Square. It was hard work but no more difficult than the begging we had been doing — and far more lucrative.

On profitable days I was able to bring something special for Mrs. Lodzia. I sometimes dealt with Hungarian soldiers, which gave me access to Hungarian cigarettes — far superior to the Polish products — as well as sardines and occasionally a good bottle of wine or brandy. Whenever I got my hands on those or any other uncommon items, I brought them to her apartment and we shared in the treat.

There were other benefits to my association with the cigarette sellers. One was the acquisition of false identity papers; I was finally able to document the existence of Janek Jankowski, my non-Jewish alias. Irving was connected to the Jewish underground, the Jewish resistance fighters who had survived the uprising, and they had papers made up for all of us. Those documents gave us much-needed security.

The only Jewish grown-up I had regular contact with was a gentleman in his late thirties or early forties we called the "Amchu Man." [1] He managed to survive in the most incredible way. He had dug a hole in the ground in a bushy field not far from our neighbourhood, a hole eerily similar to a grave. He covered it with a board, on top of which he laid some soil. He just left a tiny opening for air and light.

Like a nocturnal animal, the Amchu Man would emerge after curfew and look for food in garbage cans — knowing he could be killed if caught by the night patrols. He had no choice. The Nazis would have picked him up within minutes of showing his face in public during the day due to his Jewish appearance.

To help him, I used to go to the gas company, where the workers would get cheap meals in a subsidized cafeteria. I brought two empty cans and asked if leftovers could be poured into them. They often pitied me and gave me the soup. I would run the soup over to the Amchu Man and give him one can while I consumed the contents of the other. The Amchu Man enjoyed more than just the soup on those occasions. I was someone to talk to, which everyone needs to stay sane. I learned that he had been deported with his wife and children to the Dachau concentration camp. Somehow he managed to jump off the train, but the rest of his family were not so lucky. He ended up in Saska Kępa, and had been hiding underground for months since escaping.

In late 1943, my friendships with the Amchu Man and my cigarette-selling friends provided the structure to my life that I needed. I had a home and a place to work. The Germans were slowly losing the war. Survival seemed possible.

---

1 "Amchu" is a common word used in both Yiddish and Hebrew and found in the daily prayers, literally meaning "your people." During the Holocaust, the word became a code for covertly identifying fellow Jews.

I became too confident as life started to improve, causing me to make a few serious mistakes at that time. One involved an elderly woman on Grochowska Street. I had known her since Eli and I stayed with the Slawcias on that street. This woman, who must have been close to eighty years old, was a close friend of the Slawcias, so she knew we were Jewish but kept the information to herself.

I would drop by to visit her. She would give me some food, and every now and then I would bring her a gift. She was an extremely religious Catholic and would entertain me with long sermons — it was almost like she was some kind of prophet. Once she gave me a long speech about the Old Testament, as she called it, and how it was more important than the New Testament. She said that the Jews were God's chosen people and that despite what was happening in the war they would be the last people left on Earth when it came to an end. Another time she told me that God was going to punish the Nazis, and the Jews would get their revenge. I found her speeches uplifting. Whether they were true or not was another matter, but they sure made me feel good.

A few times she let us play with her teenaged grandson and granddaughter, when they were also visiting. One time, she left them alone with another Jewish friend and me, and we all decided to play poker. Within an hour, the girl lost all her money but wanted to stay in the game. Her brother told her the only solution was to pay us "in other ways" to earn the necessary złotys to keep playing. She could have quit to avoid the humiliation, but insisted on doing whatever was required to continue.

Because I was considered the experienced one, I went into the other room with her in exchange for a few złotys. When we resumed playing, she lost those quickly and then my friend took his turn. She lost again and then went away crying. We had behaved horribly — I don't know if we had forced ourselves on her, but we didn't give her much choice either. We left in a hurry. Although the girl's brother was a jerk who thought the whole thing was a funny joke, I was worried about repercussions from the rest of her family and never risked returning to that street. I am still sorry for what we did to that girl.

Not long after that experience I made another big mistake that almost cost me my life.

By working daily in Three Crosses Square I got to know a few Polish youths who hung out there, including two brothers who became good friends of mine. They were among the precious few gentiles who knew I was Jewish. I came to trust them after I discovered they were sympathetic to the plight of the Jews. Their father had even helped several Jews during the war. The only problem with these boys was that they were extremely wild, and in that sense were a bad influence on me.

One day when Mrs. Lodzia was away and I was alone with her daughters, I ill-advisedly invited the boys to drop by our apartment. They arrived full of energy, telling me about a German soldier who had raped a Polish woman and her daughter. The two women were friends of the boys' family, and the brothers said they couldn't let the crime go unpunished. They described how they had found out that he was in a local bar, so they went there and waited for him to come out. When he emerged half-drunk, they followed him home. On the way, they cornered him in an alley and shot him twice in the leg.

How they got that gun I'll never know — but there it was. They had brought it over to show me. The weapon was loaded when they put it in my hands. I was trembling as I gripped it. I said I was afraid of killing someone, but they just laughed, telling me the safety latch was secure so there was no danger. They kept prodding me — and for some stupid reason I pointed the gun at Irka. I knew the lock was secure, so pointing it seemed harmless. I went to pull the trigger in a mock act of shooting her and fortunately moved the gun just to the right at the last possible moment. The safety latch was not on, and the gun fired a loud pop. The bullet narrowly missed hitting her and went into the wall.

I was struck with panic. I immediately dropped the gun to the floor, dashed out of the house and just kept running. I knew no one had been injured, but I felt I had irreparably damaged my good standing with Mrs. Lodzia. I was full of guilt and extremely angry with myself. After all Mrs. Lodzia had done for me, I had nearly killed her daughter. There was no way I could ever go back to her place.

I walked around in circles all afternoon replaying my reckless behaviour in my mind. Evening approached and I wasn't sure what to do next. I was upset and really needed a friend, so I went to visit Zbyszek.

Zbyszek was my best friend in the group. He was a couple of years older than me, so he was a little bigger than most of us. He had a powerful presence, exemplified by his sharply sarcastic sense of humour. He would make jokes about death and dying that would often seem inappropriate, but it was just his way of dealing with the insanity of our lives. He was also incredibly tough. One time, a Polish youth — a big boy, about eighteen or nineteen years old — came up and threatened us.

"You two are Jews, aren't you?" the boy snapped at us. Whenever I heard the word Jew like that it felt as though a bullet was going through my heart.

"I want all your money and all your cigarettes," he continued, "or I'll give you away to the Germans."

Zbyszek stood right up to the boy who was twice his size.

"You've got quite a nerve calling us Jews," Zbyszek fired back. "We're not going to give you a single groszy. You just go ahead and call the Germans and we'll see what happens."

The boy tried to say something, but Zbyszek wouldn't stop:

"You may be older than us, but you sure have a pea for a brain. Why are you threatening the two of us? Between us, we could beat your head in. And you know, maybe that's what we'll do."

Zbyszek then pulled out a knife he used for eating and pointed it at the boy. That shmaltzer turned around and ran for his life. Zbyszek had extricated us from that predicament, but we still had to flee immediately and stay away from working in that neighbourhood for a long time. We couldn't take the chance that we might see him again. He could have run straight to the Germans. I'll never know because we never came across him again.

Like me, Zbyszek had lost his entire family. He spoke fluent Polish, had shrewd business instincts and with his blond hair and round face he didn't look at all Jewish. He used those attributes fully in developing into quite a ladies' man. He sold cutlery at the market from a blanket on the ground, which brought him into contact with many girls.

The day I almost shot Irka, I arrived at his spot in the market as a nervous wreck.

"What's up, Janek?" he asked casually.

I told him about what had happened and his mood changed entirely.

"How could you do that?" he demanded. "You've really screwed yourself."

"I know, I know," I told him. "But there's nothing I can do about it now. What's done is done. The fact is that I'm back on the street again and need a place to sleep. Where are you sleeping these days? Can I stay with you tonight?"

"Sure you can. I'm staying in the attics — rent-free. There's lots of room there, but no running water or toilets," he joked, as his mood softened again.

I could have gone with the other cigarette sellers. Most of them stayed together in one place, but I hated it there. It was a house where this unstable older woman rented rooms to drunks and other street people for ten złotys a night.

Our friends' apartment there was a pigsty. There was sooty dirt everywhere. Worse than that, the owner had a daughter who kept animals such as rabbits — and they would be running around all over the place. I stayed there one time, and when I left I was so flea-bitten that I was red and itchy for two weeks. I vowed that I would never stay there again. To me, life on the streets was better than that disgusting place. I never could understand how my friends put up with it. Zbyszek was the only other one who hated it enough to avoid going there — though he also just preferred to be on his own.

Zbyszek had chosen an apartment building in an affluent area not far from where Mrs. Lodzia lived for us to sleep in that night. We arrived there just before curfew and went straight to the attic. I got settled into a potato bag I had brought; Zbyszek lay down on a straw mat that he took with him wherever he went.

We felt relatively safe and comfortable. But there was one problem. After curfew, the front doors automatically locked, so we were committed to staying there through the night. There was no way out if we ran into trouble.

We lay there quietly for a while — speaking in a soft whisper and not letting ourselves fall asleep so early that our loud snoring might give us away. Late into the night, when we felt confident that everyone else in the building had gone to bed, we planned to have a short sleep.

About an hour after we had settled in, we heard footsteps and the voices of two women getting nearer and nearer. Step by step, they climbed the stairs toward us. Before we could do anything, they unlocked the door and entered. Each was holding a basket of wet, washed clothes, which they had brought to hang to dry in the attic.

They screamed when they saw us. "Oh my God! What are you doing here? Are you Jews?" they asked.

We maintained our poise, politely but firmly denying we were Jewish. We explained that we were two farm boys who had come to the big city for a day of fun — and that we had had so much of it that we lost track of time. Zbyszek said that the curfew was upon us and that since we didn't have enough money for a room, there was nothing we could do but sleep in this attic. I added that we would be gone first thing in the morning because we had to get home and take care of the cows.

The two women didn't believe us.

"You are Jews, aren't you?" one of them insisted. "You're hiding from the Germans and that's why you're here."

We vehemently denied it.

"We're as gentile as you are," I protested. "Do you want us to recite some prayers to prove it to you? Our father who art in heaven, hallowed be thy name…."

"Okay, okay," she said, before I could recite the rest of the prayer. "I see that you could be Christians. So where are you boys from anyway?"

We told them our stories of being from Wrocław. My parents were dead so I lived with my grandmother, who was so strict she would hit me if I didn't do exactly as she ordered. I finally ran away and ended up at a farm about thirty kilometres from Warsaw, where I worked with cows.

Zbyszek then gave his story. He said that his father was an alcoholic who beat him constantly. He couldn't take it anymore, so he ran away too. We both found work at the same farm, which had posted a help-wanted sign.

"Poor boys," the other woman said. "You must be really hungry. After we hang our laundry, we'll bring you some food."

We said that the offer was greatly appreciated and thanked them for their kindness. They quietly hung their laundry, smiled at us as they picked up their pails and said they'd be back soon with some food. They locked the door on their way out.

We were uneasy about the situation. At first, they seemed convinced we were Jews; then they said they believed our story and were going to give us food. It just didn't feel right, but there was nothing we could do. We were locked in. All we could do was hope the women had really believed us.

Ten minutes later we heard people coming up the stairs again. This time the footsteps were heavier. The door opened and we saw two men. They looked intimidating — tall and muscular, with rugged-looking faces.

"What are you doing here?" they demanded. "Why are you sleeping on the floor like two drunks? Why did you pick this place? You told our wives you're from a farm but what's the real story?"

We rehashed the same explanation over and over again — insisting that every word we told their wives was true. We assured them that we were genuinely good boys who would not steal from them and that we would be gone first thing in the morning.

"All right, we believe you," the one man finally said. "But you'd better be gone by sunrise and you'd better leave this place as clean as when you arrived — no urinating."

We promised to do as we were told. We thanked them for their kindness, telling them that God would reward them for their good deed. Their wives then handed each of us a sandwich.

"I hope we didn't get it wrong and we're actually feeding two Jew-boys," the man said with a cocky smirk on his face. "Let's go," he said to the others.

They said goodnight to us while closing the door behind them. We were worried that they had given us sandwiches laced with poison, but nothing was happening to either one of us as we ate them.

"We're still alive, so I guess the food was safe," Zbyszek said. "That's a good sign."

Nonetheless, we knew we were in trouble. The way those men talked to us made it clear they didn't believe our story. We were worried sick that they were going to come back. I was furious with myself. My life was in danger because of my bad behaviour. If only I had acted responsibly, I'd have been sleeping safe in Mrs. Lodzia's home.

A few hours later, we heard footsteps climbing the stairs. These did not sound the same as before. These were much heavier, louder — and there were more of them. We knew several people were coming for us, and we were terrified.

When the door opened, I saw a flashlight in one hand and a gun in the other. There was a moment of eerie silence and then I heard a deep Polish voice say, "Get up, Jews."

Our worst fears had been confirmed.

Brief Respite

There were four men — two German gendarmes and two Polish policemen. All four had their guns drawn and pointed at us. We were scared stiff. Fortunately, when they realized they were just dealing with two dirty little kids, they put their guns away.

"You're both Jews — rotten Jews, aren't you? Answer the question," the one Polish policeman demanded. That man was particularly nasty.

"No, no, no!" we pleaded. "We already told those others that we are gentile boys from the country." After we repeated our story two or three times, the hate-mongering Pole said he didn't believe a word of what we were saying. His reply was that if we really wanted to prove our identity we had to pull our pants down.

"If you're not circumcised, you're not Jewish, and we'll let you go," the Pole said. "If you are, then we'll know you're Jewish and we'll deal with you accordingly."

Rather than pull my pants all the way down, I just unzipped my fly, put my hand in and pushed some skin over the top of my penis to make it look uncircumcised. Wise to what I was doing, he yelled at me to pull my hand away.

One of the Germans moved forward. He had been standing quietly off to the side talking to the other German. He must have been a *Volksdeutscher* who understood Polish, because he seemed to be following exactly what was going on, translating what was being said into German for his colleague. I understood what he was saying because Yiddish — my native language — is similar to German.

In German, the officer told the Polish policemen to leave and that he would take care of us himself. The cold-hearted Pole pleaded with him, insisting that we were Jewish. But the German pretended he didn't understand a word the Pole was saying and waved the two of them off.

Once the two Poles left, he turned to his German colleague and told him that we were not Jews, just orphans looking for a place to stay. We didn't understand it, but this Nazi seemed to be saving our lives — at least for the moment.

The Germans took us down the stairs, out of the building and onto the street. We walked several blocks in the direction of a street-car stand. By then it was just about morning, and we could hear passersby callously yelling, "There are two Jews to be shot!"

We were cold, barefooted, lightly clothed, dirty and tired — and we did not know what was going on. Were we being taken to be shot? Were we going to a concentration camp? Were we being saved?

We arrived at the Kierbedź Bridge stop and waited there. The #25 streetcar came by, but we didn't take it. A few minutes later, the #26 arrived and we got on. We sat up at the front — the section for Germans only.

The #26 went through the Jewish cemetery, so I figured we were being taken there to be shot. Before we got that far, we disembarked at the Gestapo headquarters.

After going through the main entrance, we went straight to a commander's office. The Germans who brought us here greeted their grey-haired boss with the "Heil Hitler" salute, and the man saluted back. The commander asked if these were the two Jews in hiding. The German who brought us there replied that we were not Jews. He repeated our story, saying we were Polish orphans from Wrocław. He recommended that they place us in an orphanage.

I could not believe it. This man really was doing his best to save our lives. As happy as I was, however, I couldn't show any emotion. We needed them to believe we didn't understand what they were saying.

The commander signed a couple of papers and picked up the phone to make a call. A few moments later, a guard came to pick us up. He took us to a jail cell and gave us some food. An officer came several hours later to unlock it, asking which one of us was Janek and which was Zbigniew, Zbyszek's Polish alias.

"You're on your way to an orphanage," the officer said. "And it's a really nice one with good food and schooling. You two are lucky boys. There is a long waiting list to get into that place."

It sounded like a dream! I wondered if maybe I really was dreaming.

As we left, the officer told us not to run away. We walked freely beside him to a streetcar, which took us to Leszno Street, where the orphanage was located. He had papers in his hand with the stamp of approval from the Third Reich on the front page as well as a signature from the Gestapo commandant.

He took us into the orphanage, where he handed us and our papers to the priest who managed the place. The officer wished us good luck and told us to behave ourselves or he'd be back for us. We assured him we would be good.

What a break. That morning, we had figured we were dead. Now, we were in heaven — a clean, warm bed and ample food. And it was all because of that German. I'm sure he knew we were Jewish but for some reason he had saved us.

The priest told us the nurse would give us haircuts, and then we'd be able to take a bath and change into some orphanage uniforms and clean socks. Once we were cleaned up, he gave us a quick written test to assess our academic standing. He said I was at a Grade 4 level and that I would start as a pupil in that grade. Then he told us our schedule. Each day we would be up at 6:00 a.m. for a shower. Then we would go to the chapel for prayers before eating breakfast. From 8:00 a.m. until noon we would have classes. Lunch would be until 1:00 p.m., after which we would return to class until 3:30 p.m. We would have time to play games and do our homework until 5:30 p.m. Then it was time for supper, before going to the chapel for more prayers at 7:30 p.m. We had to be in our beds by 8:00 p.m., with lights out by 8:30 p.m.

"Is that understood?" he asked.

"That sounds just fine," we said.

We were introduced at supper time to all the other orphans, about thirty boys, aged eight to fifteen. We sat at a table with regular forks and knives and a napkin. The food was delicious, though it was a little strange to have to thank Jesus before and after the meal.

I got along well with the priest, who took a liking to me right from the start. Within my first couple of days in the orphanage, he asked if we had taken first communion. Being three years older than me, Zbyszek said he had. I told the priest I had not, and he saw that as a wonderful opportunity. He relished the chance to ready me for the big occasion. He got me singing in the choir and gave me postcards with pictures of Jesus on them — which I hung over my bed like a good Catholic boy.

After about a week of preparation I went to first communion. I felt extremely odd. It was one thing to masquerade as a non-Jew, but quite another to take communion.

Despite the discomfort of having Catholicism shoved down my throat, it was heaven on earth there, masking what was happening in the outside world; from inside the orphanage, it didn't even seem like there was a war going on.

Then, less than two weeks later, it all came to a sudden end.

We were inspected twice a week by the orphanage nurse after our showers to see if we had washed well enough. The nurse made sure we had no infections or wounds. Zbyszek and I would slip past her after our showers, but one morning she called me over.

"Janek, why are you always avoiding me?" she asked. "Is there some kind of problem?"

"No, there is no problem," I replied. "I am just shy and not comfortable having a woman look at my nude body. That's all. Besides, I'm not a two-year-old. I'm perfectly capable of washing myself. Don't you think so?"

"No, not at all," she said sternly. "I am the nurse and I see who I want when I want. Do you understand?"

This woman was incredibly tough, and I knew better than to aggravate her. She told me to hold up my hands and proceeded to thoroughly examine me.

"Now I know why you've been avoiding me," she exclaimed. "You are a Jew and you don't belong here. I can see you are circumcised."

"I am not a Jew," I retorted. "What do you mean by circumcised?"

She said circumcision was what separated Jews from gentiles — that on the eighth day of life Jewish boys had their foreskins removed.

"Oh that," I said. "Well, when I was little I fell on a nail and I had to go to the doctor and have it fixed. He did a good job on it, don't you think?"

She looked a little confused by my reply, and just told me to get dressed.

About fifteen minutes later, I heard an announcement over the loudspeaker: "Janek Jankowski, please come down to the doctor's office immediately."

I had a sinking feeling in my stomach that I was in major trouble. If only that nurse had some human feeling, she could easily have just forgotten the whole thing, but because of her I was terrified, unsure about what to do.

Over the next few minutes, as my name was repeated two more times, I searched for and found Zbyszek. I told him what had happened and asked him what he thought I should do. He said to go up to the doctor's office, hear what she had to say, and then decide what to do. I agreed that seemed to be the most prudent approach, so I reluctantly went up to the doctor's office. I was taken in right away.

There was a female doctor sitting at her desk. Like the nurse, she was all business and got right to the point: "Janek, Nurse Basia just told me that after examining you in the shower, she has come to the conclusion that you have been circumcised and that you are Jewish. Drop your pants down and let me have a look. I will be the final judge in this matter."

I did as she ordered, and she carefully inspected me in silence. After a few moments that seemed to take ages, she finally said something.

"Nurse Basia was absolutely correct. You are a Jewish boy."

I expected her to come to that conclusion and had given some thought on how to counter her accusation. I told my story about the nail again and added another line of argument to bolster my defence.

"Doctor, you are a smart woman. If I am Jewish, why would I have arrived here hand-delivered by the Germans with all the necessary documents? If I was a Jew, they would have shot me."

"That may be so," she said. "Nevertheless, you have been circumcised and therefore you are a Jew. As to what happened to get you here, I will look into it."

I tried one last time.

"Look doctor, is it not possible that falling on a nail would require an operation that would result in a different-looking penis?"

"Yes, that is true. But you are cleanly circumcised. There was no accident."

That was the end of the argument.

I got my stuff together and dashed down the stairs. Zbyszek was anxiously waiting for me.

"What happened up there? What did she say? Tell me, are we in trouble?" he asked, realizing that they'd soon call him to the office and see that he too was circumcised.

"We're in trouble," I replied. "She didn't believe a word of the story I gave her. I think the only thing to do now is to get out of here before the police show up to arrest us. This time we won't be so lucky. She's probably calling them right now."

Moments later we jumped over the gate in our light uniforms and ran off as fast as we could. We searched through hanging laundry in a nearby neighbourhood and eventually found some shirts and pants that fit us.

We were getting hungry as daylight started to fade. We had no money. We made it to a small store just before closing time and asked if they had any bread they could spare for two poor children. They were just about to throw out some day-old bread and gave it to us instead.

Soon after, we stumbled upon a nearby park and decided to stay there. Exhausted, we fell asleep quickly. We were once again worrying about getting caught while we slept, as had happened a couple of weeks earlier. What a turnaround we had experienced in a matter of just a few hours. We had thought we were safe with a warm bed to sleep in and good cooked meals; all of a sudden we were back where we began. I was thinking about what awful people the nurse and the doctor were. Their professions were to help people, but all they wanted to do was get us killed. On the bright side, however, at least we were free and alive. We had a peaceful night of sleep during an unusually warm autumn evening.

The next morning we decided to split up. Zbyszek had a few places to turn to and ended up doing business in the market again. A few weeks later, he was taken in by a local family.

I realized there was only one thing I could do. I had to go back to Mrs. Lodzia's and hope she would forgive me. I owed it to her to let her know how sorry I was for what I had done. I jumped onto the tail of a streetcar going to Saska Kępa and was on my way.

When I got to her doorstep, my heart was pounding like crazy. I knocked and she opened the door.

"Oh my God," she said. "I'm so happy to see you. We were sure you were dead!" She was so excited to see me. She hugged me and brought me inside.

"Where have you been for the past two weeks? How could you not let us know where you were? That was not fair of you, Janek."

"Let me explain," I interrupted. "Let me tell you everything and then you'll understand that it wasn't my fault."

I told her about the boys and the gun and apologized for my actions. She said Irka had told her all about it and that it was old news. She was more interested in what had happened to me since then.

She was shocked when she heard about my adventure. As I was finishing my story, she told me she wanted to make me something to eat. She invited me to continue staying at her place.

I said that I was grateful but would only stay if the girls still wanted me there. When they came home from school and saw me, they reacted just as their mother had — they jumped all over me with enthusiasm. They called me a cat with nine lives after I told them about my past two weeks, but I'm not sure that's true. After all I had been through between 1939 and the end of 1943, I think I escaped the clutches of death many more than nine times.

Fortunately, with the Germans losing ground to the Soviets every day, 1944 looked like it would be a better year for me. But my Nazi nightmare wasn't over yet.

A Heart in Darkness

If not for the war, I would have been preparing for my bar mitzvah during the first few months of 1944. But that was a distant dream. Life on the street was the only reality I knew.

Surviving was not easy, but I had grown accustomed to my circumstances and found street life at the later stages in the war to be much more manageable than the earlier days of smuggling myself into and out of the ghetto. I had fake identity papers to show when necessary in Three Crosses Square, as well as a special pass to ride the streetcars, which I used to travel between my work selling cigarettes and my home with Mrs. Lodzia in Saska Kępa.

As the weeks passed, I became better at selling and began to take in more money. One of the secrets of my success was a tall blond woman I met in the Three Crosses area. She worked in a nightclub that provided entertainment for the Germans. I think she was a prostitute. Her clients would pay her with cigarettes — far more than she would ever need. At least once or twice a week, she would walk past me carrying a particular handbag, which was her signal to me that I was to go to her apartment building. She would let me up to her apartment where I would purchase high-quality cigarettes from her. I bought them at dirt-cheap prices and then sold them for a large profit.

That kind of business success made me feel more confident about my chances of actually surviving the war. However, life was still extremely dangerous. The fate of a couple of my cigarette-selling buddies reminded me of this.

A boy we called Kulas, which roughly translated means someone who limps, was turned in by some shmaltzers and taken away to the Gestapo headquarters. We never saw him again. He was likely shot.

Then there was the sad end of another boy we called Francuz, or Frenchy. Even though his family was of Polish origin, Frenchy was from Paris, France. He arrived in Warsaw after escaping the Poniatowa forced labour camp. He was the last remaining member of his family.

Before the war, his parents had befriended a German official who lived in Paris. One day in spring of 1944, Frenchy saw that same man near Three Crosses Square. The officer presented himself as a long-lost friend and invited Frenchy to his place for a visit. When Frenchy got there, the man took him to the Gestapo headquarters. The boy was never seen nor heard from again.

Those were the worst of times in 1944, but there were some great moments too. The best of all came on April 22 when I celebrated my thirteenth birthday. Remembering how awful my twelfth birthday had been, I was determined to have a good time, and I can thank Mrs. Lodzia for making it happen.

I wanted to have a birthday party, something I hadn't experienced since I was eight years old. I didn't think it should be at our apartment, which would be dangerous, but all my friends were nagging me to ask Mrs. Lodzia anyway. They were more desperate for a party than even I was! Somehow, they talked me into asking her.

To my surprise, she agreed to the idea but set some conditions for it. All my friends had to arrive one at a time at ten-minute intervals and leave the same way. And everyone had to keep relatively quiet to not arouse any suspicion.

Mrs. Lodzia made cabbage rolls and sauerkraut, and each of the gang brought something with them — vodka, sausages, buns and fruits. Someone even brought a cake.

The evening started with Irving saying some prayers. We had a wonderful time. I expended so much energy that I was exhausted (and a little drunk) and fell asleep before the end of the evening. The boys played a trick on me by placing hard-boiled eggs under my bottom, which gave me quite a surprise when I awoke.

The next morning everyone left the same way they had arrived: one by one, ten minutes apart. The party was a night to remember for the rest of our lives — and it was possible because Mrs. Lodzia had such a big heart.

Mrs. Lodzia took another major risk that spring to help our friend Stasiek — the one we called Golec. He was about eighteen years old and the toughest of the group, even tougher than Zbyszek. Golec had a valuable role to play: he could keep the shmaltzers away.

As the war outlook became less promising for them, the Germans began rounding up Poles to transport to Germany so they could have additional labour for their factories. I was safe from this because I looked so young. Golec, however, appeared to be in his twenties and was picked up in Three Crosses Square. We thought we would never see him again — that the Germans would interrogate him and ultimately discover his identity and shoot him. But the Germans did not even consider that he might be Jewish. They were anxious for labour and figured he was Polish, so they shaved his head and hastily sent him away to work. Somehow Golec escaped and came back to Warsaw.

With his shaved head, he could easily have been spotted and identified by the Germans. He desperately needed a place to hide. When I told Mrs. Lodzia about his predicament, she suggested I bring him to her place and she would hide him for a few days. Golec ended up staying with us for a week. We got him a toupée and a fake moustache so that not even his mother would have recognized him. When he re-emerged, he protected himself by leaving Saska Kępa and working the streets of another district.

By the late spring and early summer of 1944, Germany did more than just take young men away for labour. More Germans were being brought into Warsaw; the Germans in the city were making themselves more visible and were becoming much more oppressive toward all Poles, who were gaining confidence as the Soviets drew closer on the Eastern Front. Under these tougher conditions, I was lucky to have Mrs. Lodzia's apartment as a haven, because it would have been more difficult than ever to be sleeping in parks and attics. The only advantage to the situation was the opportunity to make some extra money. As the war turned sharply against the Germans, newspapers became increasingly popular, and I spent more time profitably selling them than I did selling cigarettes.

On August 1, 1944, Soviet advance patrols neared the eastern suburbs of Warsaw. From Mrs. Lodzia's neighbourhood, we could hear shelling in the distance. It was difficult to contain our excitement thinking that any day we could be liberated. The Poles also felt this way. Confident that they would receive help from the Soviets, a spirited Polish uprising was launched that day to take the city back from the Germans. The Poles enjoyed some early success, quickly gaining control over most of central Warsaw.

But their early success masked a serious problem. The Polish resistance was being led by the Polish organization the Armia Krajowa, or Home Army, which was allied with the British-backed Polish government in London. The Armia Krajowa leadership was nearly as anti-Soviet as they were anti-German. Not surprisingly, the Soviets didn't support this army and were furious with the Polish populace for embracing them.

The Soviets decided to slow their progress and let the Poles and the Germans kill each other in Warsaw. England tried some independent airdrops to help the Poles but most of the supplies fell into German hands.

The Germans moved reinforcements into Warsaw and soon realized the Poles were on their own. The Germans mercilessly pounded the city. The battle between the Poles and the Germans was restricted to west of the Vistula River, so we were lucky to be in Saska Kępa, which was on the eastern edge of the river. The bridge into the city had been bombed, so we found ourselves literally metres from the war zone but relatively safe in our suburb, with the Soviets quietly waiting off to the east of us.

The main problem for us was that with the fighting, food was becoming scarce and much more expensive. Our dire need for food prompted me to go on a little adventure one day in late August. My two Catholic friends (the ones who had previously shot the German) told me that in Małkinia Górna, which was about a hundred kilometres to the east (near Treblinka), lard could be exchanged for cigarettes. I knew we needed a lot of lard at home and that any excess would be in such great demand that I could sell it to make enough money to buy a good amount of other essentials.

I asked Mrs. Lodzia what she thought of my idea and she just shrugged her shoulders. She said that I was my own boss who could decide for myself what to do. I agreed, so without much hesitation I chose to go. I reasoned that it would only be for four days, that it could be a fun adventure and that, most important of all, I could really help Mrs. Lodzia and her daughters.

We left that day, jumping on a cattle car for the journey. I felt sad on that trip. The train we were riding was probably one that was previously used to transport Jews to Treblinka — including my brother and sister. I felt awful the whole way there, but once we got to our destination I was able to put those horrible thoughts behind me and focus on the job at hand.

After sleeping outdoors for the night, we acquired the lard early the next day. With fifteen kilograms of the stuff for each of us to take back to Saska Kępa, we anxiously went to catch a train home. However, when we arrived at the station we found that the trains weren't running because the Soviets were nearing Małkinia.

The weather was really hot; if we had to wait too long for the trains to start running again, the lard would rot, so we quickly decided to return on foot. As we started walking toward Warsaw, I realized I was in for an extremely difficult journey. Unlike the other two stronger, older boys, I was small for a boy of thirteen. I struggled to keep up in that heat and humidity and with so much lard on my back. We must have covered about half the distance on the first day before we mercifully slept in a field for the night.

We got up early the next morning hoping we could finish the journey by nightfall. But the advancing Soviet army was quickly catching up to us. We could hear artillery explosions and see planes overhead. We had to run for cover when the fighting got really close, and a farmer took us in just before the shelling intensified. We emerged when the explosions stopped and saw the Soviet army in a nearby village. I felt absolutely euphoric. How I had longed to see the day the Germans would be defeated. I kept telling myself I was finally free.

Unfortunately, that assessment was premature.

The enemy returned with a blistering counter-offensive, and six hours later the territory was again in German hands. I didn't know it at the time, but the reason the Germans regained the land wasn't just because of the strength of their firepower, as I had assumed. The Soviets had voluntarily withdrawn as a result of their displeasure with the Polish uprising in Warsaw.

After the fighting subsided, we resumed our trek to Saska Kępa. We had to pass through German lines — the Germans were dug into positions and had their machine guns pointed at us as we walked down the street. We were fortunate they let us pass without incident.

Several hours later, I made it to Mrs. Lodzia's apartment.

"I was so worried about you," she said. "We heard the Soviets were advancing and that the trains had stopped running. I wasn't sure you'd be able to make it back."

"Nothing is going to happen to me," I reassured her. "I feel quite fine. And how are the girls?" I asked, demonstrating that confidence by casually changing the subject.

"Worried sick like me," she replied.

Shortly after, the mood changed for the better as everyone realized that despite my difficult ordeal I did accomplish my mission. Mrs. Lodzia kept a large portion of the lard, and I sold the rest. The excursion was worth it after all.

~

The Poles continued to be hammered by the Germans in Warsaw, with the battle raging for about two months. The Poles fought with Molotov cocktails, light machine guns and mortars. The Germans had heavy artillery at their disposal and enough soldiers to go house-to-house and room-to-room to weed out the resistance. Maybe it was the closest some Poles ever came to knowing what the past years of persecution felt like for the Jews.

By the time the uprising had ended in October 1944, the Poles had killed about 16,000 Germans. More than 150,000 Polish civilians were dead, as well as about 20,000 Armia Krajowa fighters killed and a similar number captured and taken to Germany. My friends Paweł and Zenek had been in Warsaw during the fighting. While hiding their Jewish identity, they fought with the Armia Krajowa against the Germans. They were among those taken to Germany.

With the Poles destroyed and the Germans weakened and in retreat, the Soviets were ready to begin moving in. As the Soviets prepared to resume their push, we waited patiently for liberation in Saska Kępa.

When the Soviets did make their move, we could see how the momentum was clearly in their favour. Each day, there were more Soviet planes in the air and fewer and fewer German ones. Sometimes we could watch the battles in the air — and the Germans were losing almost every one of them.

The Germans were getting licked. It was only a matter of time until we would be free. I was excited — but the Poles weren't. They hated the Soviets for conquering Poland in 1939 as partners with the Germans. I couldn't have cared less. I would much rather have been occupied by the Soviets than the Nazis.

Liberation day finally arrived in January 1945. It was somewhat anticlimactic because it seemed to have taken the Soviets forever when they could have come so much sooner. But their arrival felt wonderful nonetheless. I was no longer a hunted animal.

Playing the Right Note

My initial joy at the Soviets' arrival, however, began to dissipate. I had lived to see liberation, and the reality of my tragedy started to sink in. Life for so many years had consisted of nothing more than existing hour-to-hour and day-to-day, just fighting for survival. There was no time and no reason to consider the future. But with liberation, I had to think about what to do with the rest of my life. My family was gone, and I had neither wealth nor education as a foundation. The war had taken everything away from me. It was depressing and frustrating.

I also realized that I was lucky to be alive and that — as I told myself many times during the war — life is to be cherished and each moment seized. I had fought so long and hard for survival that I couldn't let it go to waste. I was determined to build a new life for myself. I loved Mrs. Lodzia and her family but decided it was best to leave Poland and start fresh. Warsaw had brought me nothing but heartache and sorrow, and I knew my best chance at happiness would be far away from it.

I wanted to stay in the city for a while to try to make contact with relatives who might have survived. They might be looking for me just as I was looking for them. I especially wanted to investigate my brother Getzel's fate. After fleeing to the Soviet Union, he had perhaps joined the army and was alive somewhere in the east — or maybe he had even come back to Poland as a soldier. I wrote to his old address and the Moscow Red Cross Society, but I received no response.

Mrs. Lodzia continued to give me unconditional support. She told me I could stay with her as long as I wanted and was free to leave whenever I wanted.

My next move came shortly after liberation when a Polish boy I knew introduced me to a few Jewish soldiers from the Soviet Union. The boy had served in the Armia Ludowa, the Polish People's Army. During the uprising in Warsaw against the Germans, not all the Poles had fought with the Armia Krajowa; the Armia Ludowa was allied with the Soviets instead of the Polish government-in-exile in London and the British. After liberation, soldiers from the Armia Ludowa mixed with the Soviets, who had Jews among them looking for Jewish survivors.

I was greeted somewhat reluctantly by the soldiers. They did not believe me at first when I told them I was Jewish. They asked me all kinds of questions about Judaism, and my answers only partially convinced them. They asked if I could speak Yiddish, and I told them I could but after three years of only Polish on the "Aryan" side it wasn't so easy. My brain and mouth weren't cooperating; my mind was willing and able to converse, but my mouth had other ideas. I paused for a few moments to calm down and concentrate, and over the next few minutes it all started to flow. It felt wonderful to speak my native language again, and they were finally convinced I was Jewish.

When I told them my goal was to get out of Poland, the leader of the group said I should go to Lublin, nearly two hundred kilometres southeast of Warsaw.

"The sooner you get there, the sooner you'll leave the country," he said.

I decided to leave. I had spent a few weeks unsuccessfully searching in Warsaw for surviving family members without finding a single one, so there was no longer any reason to stay. I could resume my search in Lublin for a while, and if I still couldn't find anyone but had an opportunity to leave the country, so be it.

I went to get my things together, which didn't take long. All I had were three cameras (I'm still not sure why I had three), a few toiletries, some clothes, several silver pieces and a rucksack in which to put everything. Then came the hard part — saying goodbye to Mrs. Lodzia and her daughters. I hugged and kissed the woman to whom I owe my life today. I promised her and her daughters that I would never forget them and would always remain in touch. With tears in my eyes, I headed off.

Now that I was ready to leave, there was still one problem. The trains weren't running. The railways had been demolished in the battles between the Germans and the Soviets, so I had to ask around to find another way to travel. I discovered a group of Soviet soldiers who were heading to Lublin in a flatbed military truck. They offered to let me come along.

I worried that if they discovered the three cameras in my bag they might think I was a spy. That would have resulted in getting tossed off the truck or being shot. Lucky for me, they never saw what was in my bag.

I headed straight to the marketplace when I arrived in Lublin. I needed to sell all my stuff so I'd have money for food and lodging. I didn't know how much I could get for my cameras, so I started at a high price and worked my way down until I got some takers. The clothes were easy to sell, and by the end of the day I had a good sum of złotys in my pocket.

I then went to a part of town where — according to the Jewish soldiers — some surviving Jews from around Poland had congregated. I entered a restaurant in that area; I was starving and looking forward to a special meal. I sat down and a waiter came over to serve me. He looked unimpressed by me and treated me like dirt. But I wasn't about to let him bother me. I ordered a large portion of Jewish-style roasted chicken. It was one of the most expensive items on the menu, and he asked me if I had enough money to pay for it. His eyes bulged when I took out one of the three bundles of money I had acquired from my sales in the marketplace. After that, he started treating me more like a real customer.

The restaurant had an accordion player to entertain the patrons. His name was Ludwig — Lutek in Polish. He was a deserter from the Soviet army who played music for a living. When he came to my table to see if I had any requests, I took out a few złotys and asked him if he knew the song "Treblinka." It was a sad song about the death camp, which had become somewhat of an anthem for the Jews of Warsaw. He said he knew the song and began to play it.

I started to sing along and then everyone in the restaurant turned their heads toward my table and listened intently to our rendition. Some people started to cry openly.

When the song ended, Lutek complimented me on my singing voice and asked if I wanted to work with him in the restaurant that night. I finished my meal and joined him. We had a great time, and he was quite pleased with me.

At the end of the night, he asked if I wanted to work with him on a regular basis. He explained that the restaurant was only one of several engagements at which he played. He did weddings — both Jewish and non-Jewish — and various other private parties.

I already had a plan to use my remaining złotys to go into business for myself in the marketplace. After acquiring more money, I expected to travel to a few more towns in search of relatives. I wasn't sure whether working in the marketplace or singing with Lutek would pay more, so I told him I would think about his offer and let him know in a few days.

He wouldn't accept this, however, and persisted in telling me to join him. After several minutes of his harassment, I finally agreed to work with him — but only after I took one last trip. The trains were running again, so I went to Lodz. I was there for several days, registered my name for surviving family members and bought some silk clothes, which were available there and in demand in Lublin.

Over the next few days, I came to realize the soldier who told me Lublin was the route to getting out of Poland was mistaken; any possibility to leave was still a long time away. When I returned from Lodz,

I decided to settle in Lublin for a while until the right opportunity to flee the country presented itself. I was frustrated by the wait, but at least I had a little more time to see if any relatives would surface.

Lutek had a new job playing his accordion in a mobile military hospital. He asked me to join a band he had quickly put together. His group consisted of four other wounded soldiers, who played the violin, trumpet, guitar and saxophone. They needed a drummer, and Lutek asked me if I would take on that role. Playing in a band sounded fun, so I abandoned my silk-selling ideas and joined his group. I got my hands on a set of drums and was all set to go. They even made a uniform for me. I looked just like a Polish soldier, boots and all.

I was the centre of attention wherever we would play — just a small young boy playing in a band with adults. For the most part, it was a lot of fun. I was also given the chance to sing, which I later regretted because I think it ruined my vocal cords. I was in puberty at the time and my voice was changing.

One day, not long after starting to work with them, I came down with a bad cold. I'm sure my return trip from Lodz when I had to stay on the roof of a train during pouring rain didn't help my health.

Within a couple of days my cold got much worse. Before I knew it, I was in a hospital bed suffering from pneumonia. Although antibiotics had recently started being prescribed, they weren't available yet in this hospital so I had to get by essentially untreated. The mobile military hospital was good to me. I was even placed in a room designated for officers. I pulled through eventually, but it took me weeks to fully recover.

During my illness, our hospital was ordered to get closer to the new front lines. As 1945 progressed, the Soviets were moving further into German territory, and the hospital was moved to a pretty, popular city called Sopot, on the shore of the Gulf of Danzig (now Gulf of Gdańsk).

After I was fully recovered from my illness, our band got a job playing in a Sopot nightclub, from 9:00 p.m. to 4:00 a.m. This was on top of our regular job playing for the wounded soldiers in the hospital, so we were making some decent money — but also working really hard.

I got hold of a new, better set of drums and really started to have fun with it as I became more comfortable in my role. Some of those nights were crazy. People loved our playing and would buy vodka for each of us in the band whenever we played the song "Warszawa." I drank the booze at first, but after a while I realized it wasn't doing me any good and asked the nightclub owner to bring me water instead.

In May 1945 the war in Europe had ended, and even though I was having lots of fun in Sopot, some depressing realities were keeping me from true happiness. I was not free to be a Jew. I never let on to anyone about my Jewish identity — and neither did Lutek. Antisemitism was still rampant; I would learn later that after the war pogroms victimizing the few remaining survivors were common throughout Poland. I also found out later that the much-respected head of the Sopot hospital was Jewish. She was a colonel in the Polish army who hid her Jewishness too. Neither Lutek nor I knew her real identity at the time.

The antisemitism reminded me of the true reason I was staying there. It wasn't to play songs. It was to find relatives who might still be alive, and then to leave Poland. When it became clear that I wasn't going to find any family members, I knew it was time to leave.

My goal was to be with other stranded Jews like me. I wanted to go to Palestine, to help build Israel — the Jewish nation. Unfortunately, that was easier said than done in 1945. The British weren't letting Jews in — and many who tried found themselves in detention camps in Cyprus. I decided it would be best to go to England or America and then make my way to Israel later. But first I had to get out of Poland, where any dreams of the future were destined to be quashed by nightmares of my past.

The initial promise that Lublin was a quick route out of Poland had been a setback. But eventually Lutek found out about an opportunity that seemed more promising. He too had decided it was best to leave Poland and had learned through his network that in Krakow we could pick up false papers that would gain us entry into Germany.

We got to Krakow as quickly as possible and found out that it was true — for a small fee we could have papers made up saying we were French. The plan was to get on a train to Czechoslovakia, at which time we would switch to another train that would take us into Germany. It was unclear where I would go from there, but it would be to somewhere safe outside Germany. It sounded great, but I wasn't about to get too excited until it actually materialized.

We boarded our train with our meagre belongings and set off toward Prague. Lutek spoke French, so he told me that if we got into any trouble all I had to say was "oui, oui." He would handle the rest. At the border, officials checked our papers. When Lutek asked me in French to hand mine to him so he could give both to the border agent, I said, "Oui, oui." The man looked at our documents for a second and moved on.

We changed trains and before we knew it we were in German territory. We disembarked in the city of Straubing in Bavaria. The Americans occupied that territory, so we walked to one of their main compounds. Lutek had been instructed to go see a certain major in the US military who was Jewish. The man was waiting for us.

The major told me I would be flown from Germany to England, where I would be placed in a Jewish orphanage.

I was so excited I wanted to scream. I'd soon be on my way to a whole new life.

The Gift

We flew to England in October 1945 in a plane carrying American parachutists. It was such a dramatic way to travel. I was so excited just being on an airplane — let alone a military plane that had been used to help defeat the Nazis.

I was coming to England thanks to the Central British Fund for German Jewry (now World Jewish Relief) and its Committee for the Care of the Concentration Camp Children, which sponsored the transport of a thousand orphaned children to England after the war. Along with fourteen other Jewish boys, I was placed in a hostel in the town of Northampton.

The headmaster, Isidor Marx, was a German Jew who was about sixty years old, assisted by his daughter, Esther. They worked extremely hard to help us from the moment we arrived. I was small — even shorter than I should have been — from a lack of proper nourishment during the war, so they put me on a special nutritional program to boost my growth. This worked and I grew several inches between the ages of fourteen and sixteen, though only to a final height of about five foot two.

We were well cared for in all respects. We attended a nearby public school, but I was not among the best behaved children. I'm sure I was quite a nuisance for the headmaster and his daughter. One occasion involved Queenie, their beautiful three-year-old dog, who had never been spayed. Esther didn't take her eyes off the dog when it was in heat, making sure Queenie wouldn't run away in search of a male companion. I kept telling Esther she was cruel to make the animal suffer so much. I told her she should either allow Queenie to get pregnant or spay her, so that the poor dog wouldn't be groping for a mate all the time. But Esther refused to listen no matter how often I said it.

So one evening when Esther was out for dinner, I brought a hideous-looking male dog into the hostel and let it loose on Queenie. Queenie gave birth a couple months later to six of the most unsightly puppies imaginable. Esther was livid and tried to find out who was responsible, but no one told her it was me. She gave the puppies away and finally took Queenie to get spayed.

I was also a handful for her father, who was a devoutly religious man. Although I had been raised in a strict Orthodox Jewish family, that life was a distant memory. At the hostel, I totally rejected anything to do with Judaism. Whenever he put a yarmulke on my head, I threw it to the floor. When the time came to say prayers, I refused to take part. I could not worship a God I did not believe existed.

"How could a God sentence so many innocent children to death in gas chambers?" I would ask indignantly. "How could he allow demented Germans to derive pleasure from their slaughter? If Almighty God was so wonderful and powerful, why didn't he stop the Germans before they nearly wiped out an entire people?"

I told the headmaster the sooner he accepted the fact that I would not participate in his prayer sessions, the better we would get along. I even asked to be sent to another hostel where religion wasn't practised. The man refused to give up on me, however, telling me God worked in mysterious ways and everything had happened to me for a reason. He told me that one day I would change my thinking. After I had a family of my own and did well in the world, he said, I would thank God for the gift of life.

The headmaster was a father figure to me — a kind gentleman who had an uncanny ability to connect with children. No matter how angry I became, I could never hold it against him. After talking to me daily for many months, he convinced me that my rejection of religion was just a way of venting all my anger and frustration. I did feel fortunate to be alive with a chance at a prosperous future, and I began to accept his belief that I had God to thank for it. This more positive attitude improved my outlook on everything, especially schooling. I had received only two years of a public school education in Warsaw before the war, so I faced an enormous challenge to catch up to everyone else. I applied vigorous energy to my studies. I was determined to quickly make up for lost time. I blazed through eight grades of public school in six months.

After that, I went to trade school to specialize in tool and die making, where we spent half our time learning how to use the machinery and the other half studying English, math and other academic subjects. Within two years, I completed the course work for my diploma.

In addition to my studies, the headmaster insisted I play the violin, letting me use the same instrument he played when he was a boy. I took lessons and learned a great deal, even though I wasn't too enthusiastic about it — I would have preferred to play another instrument such as the saxophone.

My lessons were paid for by a man named Mr. Rothschild, who often came to the hostel to hear what his money had produced. I would spend hours practising the pieces I had learned so I wouldn't embarrass myself. I wasn't a star but I did all right; I was good enough to play "Ave Maria" in the third and fourth positions. The moment Mr. Rothschild left, I would pack the violin away and return to the soccer field to enjoy my true love.

Toward the end of my schooling, I was transferred to a new hostel in London. I preferred it there because I could play soccer in a city-wide junior league, participate in a youth club and continue to study tool and die making at the ORT School in South Kensington. All my friends in Northampton were jealous I was able to live in the big city, especially because I could now see all the top professional soccer teams.

The headmaster at the new hostel tried to expose us to as much culture as possible, which included taking us on a tour of London on a cold and wet day. We toured museums and other sites, but I didn't enjoy it much because I had a sore throat. Over the next several days I felt worse, so a doctor examined me. He diagnosed me as having diphtheria and had me immediately rushed to the hospital and put in the isolation ward where I was treated with a new wonder drug called penicillin. I slowly recovered over the next few weeks.

Not long after that I suffered an appendicitis attack. The doctor wanted to operate on me but also told me there was a chance I could get better without an operation because the appendix was not inflamed to a crisis point. He cautioned that at some point in the future, however, surgery would be necessary because the next attack would be much more serious.

I was nervous about the surgery. I thought about how people sometimes die on the operating table — and figured that even if it were to go smoothly, it would hardly be a pleasant experience. I recalled how a friend recently had to spend two weeks in bed recuperating from an appendix operation. I felt there was no emergency yet, and if I simply reduced my physical activity I wouldn't aggravate the appendix. I think the experience of surviving the war had given me a false sense of invincibility; I actually believed that because I made it through the Holocaust, I could beat the appendicitis without an operation. I decided to put off having an operation for as long as possible, if not altogether. In the short term at least, my gamble paid off as the appendix problem soon faded away.

After I had recovered, I was happier than ever in the new orphanage. London was fascinating. Life was full of fun, with soccer games and trips to Hyde Park on Sunday afternoons to listen to people exercising their freedom of speech. It hadn't been all that long since I was struggling to survive under the cruel Nazi regime, and here I was a completely free young man with his life in front of him. But there was still that emptiness, that sadness in my heart that I would be forced to endure for the rest of my life. I had lost everyone, and now there was no one with whom I could share my exciting new life.

By the end of 1947, I was finished all my schooling and training and was ready to go to Palestine to pursue a career in a trade. The official creation of Israel was just around the corner. I now just had to be patient for a little longer until Jews would be able to immigrate there legally.

However, patience was never one of my strengths. I heard that the Canadian Jewish Congress was bringing to Canada over a thousand orphaned children who had survived the Holocaust. Children from orphanages in England were being sent, so I applied, thinking I had nothing to lose — it might be a fun move. There would be nothing forcing me to stay in Canada if I didn't like it there, so I figured I should take advantage of the opportunity to see another country in a different part of the world. I could still move to Israel after experiencing Canada for a while. It was time for a change.

To a New Life

Only ten days after applying, I was on my way. All I had to do was pass a medical exam and brief interview with Canadian government officials.

Like the other orphans going on the trip, I was excited to be going across the Atlantic on the RMS *Aquitania* — I was embarking on a great adventure on a massive ocean liner. As it departed from Southampton on January 4, 1948, all I had was forty dollars in Canadian currency, a bag full of clothes, an accordion, a violin the Northampton headmaster had given me as a going-away gift, a few school books and some photos and other memorabilia from two-and-a-half wonderful years in England.

I found myself sitting at the piano playing tunes, singing songs and drinking beer only moments after hitting the high seas. But the fun lasted all of about one hour. It took five days to get to Halifax and I was sick on each of them. With the exception of that first hour, I spent the whole trip in bed.

Five days later, a Friday afternoon, we arrived in Halifax. We were greeted by members of the city's Jewish community and a reporter from a local newspaper, who wrote about our arrival. We spent the weekend in Halifax before heading on to Montreal and Toronto.

Each of us was placed in a Jewish home for our two days on Canada's east coast. I stayed with the Zaife family. Mr. Zaife, the president of a local Jewish congregation, owned a large furniture store. He, his wife and his only daughter lived in an elegant, huge home, where I was treated like a king.

On the Saturday morning, their family maid served me the best breakfast I had ever eaten. When I was in England, eggs were rationed at one per person per week. If I was lucky, the egg was bland but edible. Often, the egg would be rotten, and I couldn't even look at it. At Mr. Zaife's house, I had four delicious scrambled eggs, a sausage, sliced tomatoes, fries and a large glass of orange juice. I had never even imagined eating a meal like that.

Mr. Zaife's eighteen-year-old daughter then took me out shopping and showed me the town. If first impressions counted for anything, Canada seemed like the greatest place in the world to live. All the people looked relaxed and worry-free, which made sense because food and anything else you might ever want seemed so plentiful.

We stopped at her father's store on the way back from our excursion. There was a souvenir shop next door, where Mr. Zaife bought a wallet for me and placed a ten-dollar bill in it as a parting gift. I still have that bill and treasure it as one of my most-prized possessions.

We left by train on Sunday night, and after dropping some children off in Montreal, we finally arrived in Toronto on Wednesday. I stayed there for a week before I was asked if I wanted to go to London, Ontario — a small city of 70,000 at the time — a two-hour drive from Toronto.

London's Jewish community had offered to absorb six boys and six girls. I was told I'd be placed in a retail fur business where I could learn the trade through an apprenticeship. I wasn't crazy about tool and die making, so this new option appealed to me. What I liked most about it was that I could follow in my father's footsteps and be a furrier just like he had been.

Becoming a furrier was an honourable route to take, though I must admit my real desire was to be able to continue my education and study music at the university level. I dreamed about being a composer and felt that was my calling in life. No one, however, was willing to give financial support for this, so I just tried to make the most out of the opportunity presented to me.

Two members of the Jewish community in London, Ontario, greeted me upon my arrival and gave me a place to stay for a week. They found work for me at Grafstein Furs, where Mr. Grafstein gave me ten dollars per week to be his apprentice. With that salary and a two-dollar-per-week stipend from the Jewish community, I was able to pay for my room and board.

I also sold my accordion and violin in exchange for a set of drums and joined a band that played at a local club. I made three-to-five times more money playing the drums three times a week than I earned in five or six days working at the fur store. Occasionally, I would play at weddings, which was the most lucrative of all — I would collect up to fifty dollars in tips from guests.

I made enough money to eat well, own a decent wardrobe and even make one of my dreams come true. I had always wanted to own a car; I saved enough to buy a used, yellow-and-black Ford. Life was better than I could have imagined, and I was pleased that I had come to London.

～

I still dreamed of immigrating to Israel. When Israel obtained its independence in May 1948, I badly wanted to go there and enlist in the army to help the country fight for its survival. But the appendix I had neglected in England came back to haunt me. After a painful attack, I required emergency surgery, and by the time I recovered the war was over. I also had to admit to myself that I was becoming quite comfortable in London, so I decided to stay and continue the life I had begun.

At the age of twenty-two, after working for six years at Grafstein's, I asked Mr. Grafstein for a ten-dollar raise on the fifty dollars I was paid each week. When he refused, I quit and opened my own store. I was confident I could run my own business because I did all the same work Mr. Grafstein did. The only difference was that he owned the store and made heaps of money, while I was poor.

I started by renting a place across the street from Grafstein Furs. That didn't please Mr. Grafstein, so he called the woman who owned the place I was renting to tell her I didn't have any money and wouldn't be able to pay the rent. I couldn't convince her otherwise, so I had to find another place two blocks away. This turned out to be for the best. I found a better place, which came with an upstairs apartment where I could live.

I carved a niche for myself by specializing in remodelling and restoring old coats. After doing some advertising, I got more work than I could handle.

Five years later, Mr. Grafstein had to sell his business after becoming seriously ill. I bought his place and expanded my business to employ eight people. Business just kept getting better.

As the years passed, I was spending sixty to seventy hours per week in the fur shop and playing in the band the rest of the time. I was working hard, but I was having fun. There was only one thing missing in my life — a family. No matter how much I enjoyed myself in Canada, I could not erase the past. My family had been taken away from me and nothing I did would ever change that. But I could start my own family. I was twenty-eight years old, and all my friends seemed to be married — several of them were already parents. With a stable foundation for a family — a house, a car, a good income — I decided that it was time to settle down. I began dating many young women but couldn't find anyone special. Then I went on the trip of my life and met the woman of my dreams.

Since the fur season would typically last from October to March, at the end of March, I would take a vacation to re-energize. In 1959, I decided to finally go to Israel for a couple of weeks in April. I wanted to visit my friends who had immigrated there, to meet their wives and see their children.

Unfortunately, just a couple of days prior to leaving I came down with a bad case of the flu. I thought about cancelling my trip but de-cided to go despite my health. After all I had been through in life, I was not someone who allowed a little illness to get in my way.

I arrived in Israel to a terrible thunderstorm with heavy rain. I took my luggage, passed through customs and hired a cab to take me to a hotel. I made the mistake of not making any reservations for my accommodations in Israel; it was the Passover holiday period, and almost every hotel room in the country seemed to be booked.

We drove around for more than two hours before we finally came upon a place in Tel Aviv where a woman told me that if I didn't mind sleeping in the lobby for a while there would be a vacancy the follow-ing morning. I accepted her offer without hesitation. I paid the taxi driver, giving him a good tip for his efforts, checked in and fell asleep on a couch at about 2:30 a.m.

When I woke up in the morning, I felt feverish and my throat was very sore. I went up to my room and asked the woman at the front desk to send a doctor to see me. When the doctor arrived, my temperature was up to 104° F. He said I had caught an extremely nasty flu. He gave me some antibiotics and said he'd check on me the next day because he had seen a woman die from the same illness earlier in the week.

I couldn't believe he told me that. I was now very worried, but each day I got a little better. After four days, I felt good enough to leave my room and eat dinner in the restaurant downstairs.

I sat at my table and ordered some cognac to drink before I ate my meal. At the table next to me was a man and a young woman in an Israeli military uniform. I remember that it was odd because they spoke Russian and not Hebrew. I wandered over and speaking mostly in English — because I didn't speak Hebrew and knew only a little Russian — I asked them why they were speaking Russian. The man spoke English and told me that they emigrated to Israel from the Soviet Union after World War II and that they still often used their native language.

They invited me to sit down with them. We spoke about where I was from and why I was in Israel. After we had dinner together, they invited me to go see a movie with them, and although I still felt weak I took them up on the offer.

Despite the language barrier, I enjoyed my time with that young woman and wanted to get to know her better. When the evening ended, all I knew was that her first name was Sonia, she was serving in the army and she was from Haifa.

The next day was Friday, so I booked a hotel in Haifa and took a cab up to the city. I explained to the cab driver that I was looking for a specific woman who would probably be at the military camp closest to the city. Because it was Friday, I knew that she would get to go home at the end of the day for the Sabbath, and I wanted to offer her a ride. The driver took me to a nearby camp, where we asked the guard if a woman named Sonia was there.

The guard summoned someone from the compound, and a few moments later a Sonia was driven by jeep to the front entrance. Unfortunately, this was not the Sonia I was looking for. I thanked the guards for their help and told the cab driver to try another camp. Then, out of the corner of my eye, I saw Sonia walking out of the gate. I yelled at the driver to stop the car. In my broken Russian, I asked her if she wanted a ride home, and she accepted.

As I dropped her off, I invited her for dinner at my hotel. She said she'd talk it over with her parents and let me know. She accepted my invitation, and when I picked her up she looked stunning, beautifully made up for a night out. We had dinner and went out to a nightclub afterwards before I took her back to her parents' place.

The next day she called to tell me she had two weeks off and could show me around Haifa that day. We had lunch and spent the rest of the day seeing the sights. We had a great time — so good that I asked her if she wanted to spend the rest of my vacation with me touring around the country. She accepted, as long as her father could come with us. I said that was fine and that we'd go the next day. I rented a car, and we had a great time with what remained of my vacation.

It may seem strange judging by today's practices, but I was convinced she was the right woman for me. It didn't matter that we had barely met; I somehow just knew that we were meant to be. The day before I was to leave Israel for Canada, I asked her if she would marry me.

To my great joy she accepted my proposal, and I delayed my departure by two weeks so we could get married in Haifa. There wasn't much time to plan the event, but we managed to make all the arrangements and had more than a hundred friends and family attend. It was a bittersweet day for me. A wedding day is naturally a joyous occasion, but it is also a time to be shared with family. I was surrounded by so many of Sonia's relations; that no one was there from my family was extremely depressing.

Nonetheless, we had a great time and excitedly went to Ashkelon in the south of the country for our honeymoon.

Then it came time for me to return to Canada. It was a tearful goodbye, but at least I knew Sonia would soon join me. She arrived in Montreal eight weeks later. I picked her up and drove her to London. Coming to Canada was such a brave thing for her to do. She was just eighteen, yet she gave up all she had known in Israel to join me in Canada where she didn't know anything about the language or culture. All she came here with was a blind faith in our love.

Our relationship motivated me to work even harder so I could make her happy after she had sacrificed so much to be with me. And although I was still not rich by any stretch of the imagination, I decided to bring Sonia's mother and three younger siblings to Canada so that she could be with her family. (Her parents had separated, so her father stayed in Israel.)

Over the following decade we had four children — three boys and a girl. I am proud that we were able to raise them in this wonderful country of Canada.

Words cannot express how happy I am that I chose to come to Canada. It was the best thing I have ever done. I have a great family here, and I have been able to live a productive life full of opportunity.

In 1998, I celebrated my fiftieth year in Canada. I have enjoyed thirty-nine years of a terrific marriage, have had the privilege of seeing my children grow up with an education and have experienced forty-five years of owning my own business.

Given everything that has happened to me — the fact that I miraculously escaped death as a young boy having witnessed nothing but pain and tragedy — I am pleased to say that because of my life here in Canada I will leave this earth as a happy man.

Epilogue

The close kinship I maintained with fellow survivors was one of the main sources of strength that allowed me to make it through the war. We were like family to each other, and one of the joys of my life was seeing several of them survive. Many of those who endured are still alive as I write my story today.

After all we had overcome during the war, it was a terrible tragedy when my closest friend, Zbyszek, died after we were liberated. A Soviet soldier shot him — I do not know any other details. I'm not sure whether he was just in the wrong place at the wrong time, or if he did something to provoke the soldier. Whatever the case, I was deeply saddened by his death. To this day I feel a sense of loss that Zbyszek, whose full name was Izaak Grynberg, did not have the opportunity to find the joy in life that I have, and that our friendship never had the chance to make it into adulthood.

Romek, another of my closest friends in our gang, also didn't survive the war. One day we were washing and playing in the Vistula at a time when the water levels were dangerously high. One of our boys called for help as he was having problems staying afloat. Romek dove out to help the boy in distress. The boy was able to grab a tree limb and get to safety, but Romek got caught in an undertow and drowned. His body wasn't discovered until the next day. The oppression we experienced hardened all of us, but Romek had somehow managed to remain the most polite, kindest boy in our group. His death was a severe blow to all of us.

Most of our group, however, did survive. Golec, the older boy Mrs. Lodzia hid for a week, came to Canada and settled in Montreal. His full name was Morris (Moishe) Wajcer, and he became a successful businessman, got married, had five children and now has several grandchildren. We were excited for him when shortly after the war he found out that his twin brother had survived in hiding. Golec is still alive, but his brother passed away about fifteen years ago.[1]

The other two brothers in our group, Paweł and Zenek, had quite a story to tell when we met up again after the war. When the Warsaw Uprising took place while I was in Saska Kępa, Paweł and Zenek were still in the city. In a display of outstanding courage, they fought with the Armia Krajowa against the Germans. Just before the war ended, they were captured and taken to Germany, where they were later liberated. In the Warsaw battles, they performed heroic acts and were decorated with medals after the war. They had to conceal their identity as Jews; when their Jewish identity was eventually revealed, they were no longer treated as heroes, despite all they had done.

After the war, they immigrated to Israel. When their new country was attacked soon after gaining independence, they fought valiantly in its defence, and soon after became high-ranking officers. Paweł, whose full name was Peretz Hochman, saw his sons continue the tradition of being officers in Israel's forces. Zenek — Zalman Hochman — also married and raised a family there. Unfortunately, he died of cancer in 1996.[2]

Many of our gang made it to Israel, including Boluś — Bencjon Fiks — who also joined the Israeli military. The Amchu Man — who had survived in his hole in the ground right up until the end of the

---

1   Morris Wajcer passed away in Montreal in 2003.
2   Peretz Hochman passed away in Israel in 2013.

war — also found his way to Israel; his real name was Aleksander Celnikier. He became a bus driver there before dying in the 1970s.

The friends who did not go to Israel are scattered throughout the world from Argentina to Australia to the United States. A few, however, such as Golec, live quite close to me. Bull, whose name was Irving Milchberg, our main connection in Warsaw for "Aryan" identity papers, became a businessman in Niagara Falls, Ontario. He got married and had two brilliant children — an architect and a physicist.[3] I also have good friends who moved to Detroit and Philadelphia in the United States.

My smuggling buddy Sewek moved to Toronto. Sewek — Sam Weizenbluth — aided me through so many difficult moments, including helping me carry my father's body from our upper-floor apartment. When we met at weddings or bar mitzvahs, we fondly discussed both our families who had lived in that dwelling in the ghetto. He lost his mother and sister in the ghetto, while his father and brother suffered an unknown fate after crossing the border to the Soviet Union.[4]

I do not know what happened to so many of the wonderful people who touched my life during the course of the war. I can only assume that the four men — Jankiel, Szlojme, Jacob and Aaron — died after leaving the ghetto. I did learn that Zlata never made it out and died when it was razed to the ground.

Perhaps most special of all during the war was Mrs. Lodzia — the woman who hid me for almost a year and a half. I could never say enough about how much that wonderful person helped me. She lived life to the fullest each day and was willing to risk her life, and her children's, so I could do the same. I was like a son to her, and she a second mother to me.

---

3 Irving Milchberg passed away in 2014.
4 Sam Weizenbluth passed away in 2013.

I stayed in touch with the Lodzia family from the day I left Poland, sending parcels and money at Easter, Christmas and for birthdays. Mrs. Lodzia died in 1978 at the age of seventy-three following a long battle with cancer. Only one of her daughters remains alive today. Marysia was fifty-six when cancer claimed her life. I still correspond with Irka, and I am touched when her children refer to me as Uncle Jankiel in their letters.

I am extremely proud of my own children: Mark, Irv, Ed and Brenda. And nearly four decades after I met Sonia, we are still happily married — enjoying life more than ever.

As I reflect on the events of my childhood, the experiences have taught me above all just how precious life is. Surviving daily misery was an education in appreciation. I learned to savour the joy of simply breathing fresh air. Eating a good meal was like being in heaven.

I feel fortunate to have led a normal life in a great country. Sometimes I find it difficult to believe I am the same person who experienced all the tragedies described in this book. The times I do think about all I went through — and the emotional scars and the guilt that still remain — I realize how lucky I am. Many other survivors could not adjust and spent the rest of their lives unable to cope.

There have been many times when it has been difficult to live with the horrors of my past. It is common for me to have terrifying nightmares of Germans chasing me or that I'm trapped in a burning hiding place.

I sometimes think about what would have happened had the Holocaust not happened. It is likely my family would have branched out to hundreds of members. What they all could have achieved had they been given the chance will forever be unknown. It is still difficult for me to understand how I could not find even a single cousin who had survived.

My sister Brenda had a wallet filled with photographs of my parents and the rest of us. What I would give for just one of those photos! The few precious photos I have left are in this book — most notable is a picture of Eli and me, taken not long before his death. It sits prominently on our family room mantelpiece. Only in my memory can I now visualize my parents, my other brothers and my sister. I never had the joy of seeing them grow up, of seeing nieces and nephews being brought into the world.

The Holocaust should never have happened. I still find it hard to grasp how Germany — such a prominent nation — could demonstrate such vicious behaviour.

In 1993, the fiftieth anniversary of the Warsaw Ghetto Uprising was commemorated in Poland. I had made plans to make the trip and see all my friends gathered there. But in the end, I couldn't bring myself to go. It would hurt too much. I can never go back to Poland. My memories of Warsaw are too sickening, vivid and filled with pain, sorrow and suffering. I feel nothing but hate and bitterness toward the place. I couldn't even visit my parents' graves because the cemetery is gone; apartment buildings have been erected where the graveyard used to be.

Jews will probably never be able to live dignified lives in Poland. Antisemitism is still very much part of the national mindset there, as it is in many other countries. Even in the most tolerant countries, such as Canada, Jew-hating still thrives. From the days of the Spanish Inquisition to the neo-Nazi movement of the 1990s, Jews have always paid a heavy price for their existence. The longer I live, the less sense it all makes to me. Why is the Jew always picked on and persecuted? Why is the Jew always the scapegoat?

It seems to me that because Jews were Hitler's target, no one raised an eyebrow.

Had the Nazis targeted another group of people, I wonder whether the rest of the world would have galvanized, would have intervened at an early stage and prevented the whole, gigantic tragedy. Just before the war, there was a boat with almost a thousand Jews aboard that sailed the Atlantic; those on board hoped the Americans or British or Canadians would offer refuge. They were rejected and forced to return to Europe where so many were murdered like all the other Jews. Neither Churchill, Roosevelt, nor any of the other supposedly benevolent leaders offered help when needed.

And who is to say another Holocaust will not occur? Perhaps we still haven't learned the lesson — as we have seen in places like Bosnia and Rwanda. If we are to prevent such terrible occurrences from happening again, those who lived through the horror must make others aware of what happened. Present and future generations must know.

It is not surprising that voluminous amounts have been written about the Holocaust. However, in less than a generation, there will be few, if any, people around who were there and who can provide first-hand accounts of what happened to them. I suspect mine will be among the last.

I have felt it is important to make my contribution. I hope this book adds a little more to the knowledge and understanding of this dark chapter in human history, so it will never again happen.

My friend Joe, the man who sent his daughter to Polish farmers and died after stabbing a German in the *Umschlagplatz*, had a saying he repeated to me to keep my spirits up as we confronted the anxiety of hiding in an attic in the ghetto. "Where there is life there is hope," he said, "and where there is hope there is life." One of the main reasons I survived the war was that I never relinquished my hope. And for the future, I must also remain hopeful. Perhaps one day the lessons of the Holocaust will truly be learned, and humankind will be able to live in a world free from the cancer of bigotry.

Afterword

The timing and some of the details are vague — I think I was seven or eight years old — but the essence of the scene remains vivid in my mind.

Yom HaShoah, Holocaust Remembrance Day, was being observed at Or Shalom synagogue in London, Ontario, where we lived. My father, as he did every year, lit one of the candles to remember the six million Jews murdered in the Holocaust. The solemnity of the moment was made even more poignant by the anguish on his face. I could see how the experience was transporting him back to the unfathomable tragedy he had endured as a boy. It was not lost on me that when the war began, he would have been about the same age as I was at the time of the ceremony.

I will never forget how my dad reacted to his painful memories the moment we stepped back from the candle. He held me close to him, gently stroked my cheek with his thumb and flashed me a quick smile.

My dad viewed his experiences during the Holocaust as an integral part of who he was. They were a fact of life not to be hidden or avoided, so his identity as a survivor surfaced naturally and often in our household. How my father acted and what he shared allowed me, at a very young age, to have a clear sense that unspeakable horrors had been inflicted on him.

And yet, as my experience at the remembrance ceremony demonstrated, he would not dwell on his memories of that time for very long. To make a point, he might make a cursory reference to his distant past. His starvation during childhood would be described to teach me to be grateful for the simple things in life. Or, to explain the importance of being constantly vigilant when navigating the wider world, he would illustrate how he had seen first-hand just how ruthless humans can be.

He never stayed in the past for very long, making a point to move quickly back to the present. That usually meant animatedly conveying how happy he was to have built a wonderful life in Canada — with a wife he cherished, children he adored and a business that drove and fulfilled him.

However, a by-product of that approach was that I grew up with limited knowledge about the actual details of his wartime experiences. For example, I knew he had been a smuggler in the Warsaw ghetto, but I did not know much about the cruel Nazi guard known as Frankenstein. I knew his siblings had all been murdered, but I knew very little about the betrayal that led to Eli's death.

That changed around the time my father turned sixty, when he told me he felt obligated to fully document his experience during the Holocaust. He said he had been thinking about it for many years but had not been able to bring himself to unpack memories that were too painful to bear. But this time, he said, he was determined to do it. This documenting of his life in Warsaw during the war, it turned out, would be done slowly over time, with notebooks recounting what he described to me as all the "episodes" of his childhood. Given that English was his third language, he asked for my help reviewing his work, to help him "put it all together." I was honoured to play that role.

As I pored over his handwritten pages, what I read made me feel sick to my stomach, and yet I was also immensely proud of his strength and courage in surviving and for his willingness to re-engage with all his trauma in such great detail so many years later.

Eventually, we reached the point where he had the makings of a complete and coherent memoir. We were thrilled in the late 1990s when the publisher Vallentine Mitchell in the United Kingdom accepted the manuscript of what we had then titled *Out of the Ghetto*. When the book was published in the year 2000, it even received some publicity, including a full-page feature in the *London Free Press* and a special display in one of the largest bookstores in London, Ontario.

Then, one evening in September of 2000, in a large meeting room in London, my father gave his one and only public talk about the book and his life. Turnout far exceeded our expectations. We ran out of chairs, forcing some people to stand at the back of the room. I had the privilege of sitting next to my father as he spoke. I did my best to offer some much-needed support and encouragement, because he was full of dread and nervousness. For days ahead of time, he told me how he wished he had said no when asked to do it.

In the end, he spoke passionately, uninterrupted for well over ninety minutes, as he relived yet again much of what was in his book. I recall how everyone listened intently, and when it was over about half the attendees came to the front to give him a hug and thank him for sharing his story.

More than an hour after his presentation ended, we were finally able to go home. We couldn't have been more than a few steps out of the building when my father told me that enduring the evening required all the strength and energy he could muster. He said that he was done talking about his experiences, that the nightmares had been coming too often, and that with the book completed and published, he had made his contribution and wanted to permanently retreat into quiet anonymity. I told him that everyone close to him — including me — could understand why he felt that way and would support the decision.

And with that, he happily continued living the life he loved so much.

In 2006, finally, and somewhat reluctantly, he closed his shop and retired at the age of seventy-five. He settled into a calmer, slower life. He played and wrote music, tended to his backyard pool, corresponded with old friends around the world, entertained neighbours and former store staff and customers, and closely followed the news, especially what was happening in Israel. Most importantly, he enjoyed doing all of that with my mom at his side and with the occasional visit from his children and their families, who lived in Toronto.

In 2013, that promise he made to himself to no longer speak publicly about his Holocaust experiences was put to the test. French filmmaker Chochana Boukhobza was working on a documentary about the Jewish boys who passed as gentile and sold cigarettes in Three Crosses Square in Warsaw, even after the destruction of the ghetto. She had already made arrangements to interview my dad's friends who were still alive. Despite that, my dad would not budge from his position, insisting that he was serious about that commitment he had made to himself almost thirteen years earlier. But with persistence from Chochana, and some annoying prodding from me, he reluctantly agreed to a brief on-camera appearance, with only a handful of questions posed to him.

I must admit I was as surprised as Chochana and her colleagues when the interview that morning lasted for about three hours. Unprompted, my dad detailed much of what is in this book. He even played some songs of Holocaust grief on the piano, after he and my mom insisted the entire crew stay for lunch. That film about my father and his friends, with footage from the period and incredible interviews, is called *Little Heroes from the Warsaw Ghetto* and came out in 2013.

Unfortunately, my father — who passed away on December 15, 2019 — lived just long enough to witness a disturbingly sharp global rise in Holocaust denial and distortion, including in Canada. I remember him telling me — going back to when I was a child and then repeatedly and unwaveringly over the ensuing decades — that antisemitism was never going to go away, and that Nazism would rise again, possibly in my lifetime, or even in his. Not long before his death, he delivered that message to me as forcefully as ever.

That's why I'm sure he would be as grateful as I am that the Azrieli Foundation's Holocaust Survivor Memoirs Program published this book, a newly edited and updated edition of his earlier memoir, in 2023, coinciding with the eightieth anniversary of the Warsaw Ghetto Uprising. My dad's story has renewed value and purpose, playing a role in the Foundation's mission to teach current and future generations about the Holocaust, at such a dangerous time when that education is so desperately needed. It is also very meaningful that his memoir has now been published in his home country of Canada.

On a personal note, I want to thank the Azrieli Foundation, and especially Matt Carrington, Arielle Berger, and their colleagues who worked on this book. Beyond channelling their considerable talents and expertise into this project, I have been struck by their kindness and thoughtfulness. In particular, they eagerly shared new information and documentation their research uncovered about my father from his teenage years immediately after the war. That was an unexpected and special gift our family will always cherish.

Ed Klajman
Toronto, Ontario

Glossary

Aktion (German; pl. *Aktionen*) A brutal roundup of Jews for mass murder by shooting or for deportation to forced labour, concentration and death camps.

Anielewicz, Mordecai (1919–1943) Polish Jewish leader of the Jewish Combat Organization resistance group, which was instrumental in the Warsaw Ghetto Uprising in the spring of 1943, and one of the most renowned individuals in the history of Jewish resistance against the Nazis. Although he had fled to Soviet-occupied territory when Germany invaded Poland, he returned to Poland and to the Warsaw ghetto to continue his work with a Zionist youth organization, in which he had a prominent role before the war. Anielewicz took over leadership of the Jewish Combat Organization in the fall of 1942 and motivated the ghetto fighters to resist the Nazis even though there was little chance of survival. Anielewicz died on May 8, 1943, during the Warsaw Ghetto Uprising when the Nazis attacked the headquarters of the Jewish Combat Organization. *See also* Jewish Combat Organization; Warsaw Ghetto Uprising.

Armia Krajowa (Polish; Polish Home Army) Also known as AK or the Home Army, the Armia Krajowa was the largest armed resistance movement in German-occupied Poland during World War II. Originally formed in 1939 as the Związek Walki Zbrojnej

(Union of Armed Resistance), the movement was renamed in 1942 and began to integrate other Polish underground forces under its umbrella. Although it has been criticized for antisemitism, and some factions were even guilty of killing Jews, the AK also established a Section for Jewish Affairs that collected information about what was happening to Jews in Poland, coordinated communications between Polish and Jewish resistance organizations, and supported the Council for Aid to Jews. Hundreds of Jews joined the AK, and members of the AK assisted the Jewish resistance during the Warsaw Ghetto Uprising in 1943. In August 1944, the AK started an uprising to liberate Warsaw from German occupation, but they were defeated in October 1944. *See also* Warsaw Uprising.

Armia Ludowa (Polish; Polish People's Army) A communist partisan force established by the Polish Workers' Party that carried out military action against the Nazis and supported a future communist-led government in Poland.

Aryan A nineteenth-century anthropological term originally used to refer to the Indo-European family of languages and, by extension, the peoples who spoke them. It became a synonym for people of Nordic or Germanic descent in the theories that inspired Nazi racial ideology. "Aryan" was an official classification in Nazi racial laws to denote someone of pure Germanic blood, as opposed to "non-Aryans," such as Slavs, Jews, part-Jews, Roma and others of supposedly inferior racial stock.

Gestapo (German; abbreviation of Geheime Staatspolizei, the Secret State Police) The Nazi regime's brutal political police that operated without legal constraints to deal with its perceived enemies. The Gestapo was formed in 1933 under Hermann Göring; it was taken over by Heinrich Himmler in 1934 and became a department within the SS in 1939. During the Holocaust, the Gestapo set up offices in Nazi-occupied countries and was responsible for rounding up Jews and sending them to concentration and death

camps. They also arrested, tortured and deported those who resisted Nazi policies. A number of Gestapo members also belonged
to the Einsatzgruppen, the mobile killing squads responsible for
mass shooting operations of Jews in the Soviet Union. In the
camp system, Gestapo officials ran the Politische Abteilung (Political Department), which was responsible for prisoner registra-
tion, surveillance, investigation and interrogation.

Jewish Combat Organization (in Polish, Żydowska Organizacja Bojowa, known as ŻOB; also translated as Jewish Fighting Organization) The main group of Jewish fighters in the Warsaw Ghetto
Uprising, led by Mordecai Anielewicz. Created by members of an
array of Jewish youth movement organizations in July 1942, the
Jewish Combat Organization was formed to resist the Nazi deportations, culminating in the Warsaw Ghetto Uprising. Using weapons smuggled from the Polish underground, the five hundred
members of the organization waged armed resistance for nearly
a month before being defeated by the overwhelming German
forces. *See also* Anielewicz, Mordecai; Warsaw Ghetto Uprising.

Jewish ghetto police (in German, Ordnungsdienst; Order Service)
The police force that reported to the Jewish Councils, under Nazi
order. The Jewish ghetto police were armed with clubs and carried
out various tasks in the ghettos, such as traffic control and guarding the ghetto gates. Eventually, some policemen also participated
in rounding up Jews for forced labour and transportation to the
death camps, carrying out the orders of the Nazis. There has been
much debate and controversy surrounding the role of both the
Jewish Councils and the Jewish police. Even though the Jewish
police exercised considerable power within the ghetto, to the Nazis these policemen were still Jews and subject to the same fate as
other Jews.

Judenrat (German; pl. Judenräte; Jewish Council) A group of Jewish leaders appointed by the German occupiers to administer the
ghettos and carry out Nazi orders. The Judenräte tried to provide

social services to the Jewish population to alleviate the harsh conditions of the ghettos and maintain a sense of community. Although the Judenräte appeared to be self-governing entities, they
were actually under complete Nazi control. The Judenräte faced
difficult and complex moral decisions under brutal conditions
— they had to decide whether to cooperate with or resist Nazi
demands, when refusal likely meant death, and they had to determine which actions might save some of the population and which
might worsen their fates. The Judenräte were under extreme pressure and they remain a contentious subject.

Organization for Rehabilitation through Training (ORT) A voca-
tional school system founded for Jews by Jews in Russia in 1880
to promote economic self-sufficiency in impoverished communities. The name ORT derives from the acronym of the Russian
organization Obshestvo Remeslenogo Zemledelcheskogo Truda,
Society for Trades and Agricultural Labour. ORT schools continued to operate through World War II. After the war, ORT set up
rehabilitation programs for the survivors, serving approximately
85,000 people in 78 displaced persons camps in Germany. Today,
ORT is a non-profit organization that provides educational services to communities all over the world.

Orthodox The religious practice of Jews for whom the observance of
Judaism is rooted in the traditional rabbinical interpretations of
the biblical commandments. Orthodox Jewish practice is char-
acterized by strict observance of Jewish law and tradition, such
as the prohibition to work on the Sabbath and certain dietary re-
strictions.

Passover (in Hebrew, Pesach) An eight-day Jewish festival that takes
place in the spring and commemorates the exodus of the Isra-
elite slaves from Egypt. The festival begins with a lavish ritual
meal called a seder, during which the story of the Exodus is told
through the reading of a Jewish text called the Haggadah. During
Passover, Jews refrain from eating any leavened foods. The name

of the festival refers to God's "passing over" the houses of the Jews and sparing their lives during the last of the ten plagues, when the first-born sons of Egyptians were killed by God.

Rosh Hashanah (Hebrew; New Year) The two-day autumn holiday that marks the beginning of the Jewish year and ushers in the High Holidays. It is celebrated with a prayer service and the blowing of the shofar (ram's horn), as well as festive meals that include symbolic foods such as an apple dipped in honey, which symbolizes the desire for a sweet new year.

SS (abbreviation of Schutzstaffel; Defence Corps) The elite police force of the Nazi regime that was responsible for security and for the enforcement of Nazi racial policies, including the implementation of the "Final Solution" — a euphemistic term referring to the Nazis' plan to systematically murder Europe's Jewish population. The SS was established in 1925 as Adolf Hitler's elite bodyguard unit, and under the direction of Heinrich Himmler, its membership grew from 280 in 1929 to 52,000 when the Nazis came to power in 1933, and to nearly a quarter of a million on the eve of World War II. SS recruits were screened for their racial purity and had to prove their "Aryan" lineage. The SS ran the concentration and death camps and also established the Waffen-SS, its own military division that was independent of the German army.

Talmud (Hebrew; study) A collection of ancient rabbinic teachings compiled between the third and sixth centuries that includes explications of scriptural law in a text known as the Mishnah and deliberations about the Mishnah in a text known as the Gemara. The Talmud remains a focus of Jewish study and the basis of traditional Jewish law and practice today.

Treblinka A Nazi death camp in German-occupied Poland about eighty kilometres northeast of Warsaw, established in 1942. Treblinka was the third death camp built specifically for the implementation of Operation Reinhard, the planned mass murder of the Jews in occupied Poland. The first massive deportations to

Treblinka were from Warsaw and began on July 22, 1942. Inmates of the camp staged an uprising in August 1943 and hundreds of prisoners escaped, but the majority of them were caught and killed. Treblinka was dismantled in the fall of 1943. Approximately 900,000 Jews and unknown numbers of Poles, Roma and Soviet POWs were killed in Treblinka.

Umschlagplatz (German) A collection point, used to refer to the areas where the Nazis assembled Jews for deportation to death camps. The term is most often used in connection to the Warsaw ghetto.

Warsaw ghetto A small area in the city of Warsaw where approximately 400,000 Jews were forced to live beginning in October 1940. Enclosed by a ten-foot wall, the ghetto's horrific conditions led to the death of 83,000 people from starvation and disease. Mass deportations from the ghetto to the Treblinka killing centre were carried out between July and September 1942.

Warsaw Ghetto Uprising A large rebellion by Jewish resistance fighters in the Warsaw ghetto, beginning on April 19, 1943, and lasting several weeks. After the mass deportation and murder of ghetto inhabitants in the summer of 1942, resistance groups prepared for an uprising. In January 1943, the Nazis attempted to deport the remaining Jews, but they encountered armed resistance and suspended deportations. When the Nazis entered the ghetto to deport the remaining inhabitants in April 1943, about 750 organized ghetto fighters launched an insurrection, while the other inhabitants took shelter in hiding places and underground bunkers. The resistance fighters were defeated on May 16, 1943, resulting in the destruction of the ghetto and the deportation of the remaining Jews; more than 56,000 Jews were captured and deported, and about 7,000 were shot.

Warsaw Uprising An uprising by the non-communist Polish resistance movement, the Armia Krajowa, to liberate Warsaw from German occupation and take control of the city before the Soviets arrived. The uprising started on August 1, 1944, as the Soviet army neared the city from the east. Facing a severe shortage of supplies and a calculated lack of support from the Soviets, the AK's approximately 40,000 troops were defeated by October 2, 1944. The revolt resulted in the deaths of over 150,000 civilians and the further destruction of a significant portion of the city. About 85 per cent of Warsaw had been destroyed by the time the city was taken over by the Soviets and the pro-Soviet First Polish Army in January 1945. *See also* Armia Krajowa.

yarmulke (Yiddish; skullcap; in Hebrew, kippah) A small head covering traditionally worn by Jewish men as a sign of reverence for God.

Photographs

1 Jack (right) and his brother Eli. Warsaw, 1943.
2 Jack in Three Crosses Square. Warsaw, 1943.
3 Jack in a decorative photo frame of the period. Warsaw, circa 1944.
4 Jack (right) with his friend Zbyszek (Izaak Grynberg). Warsaw, 1943.

1 False identity document of Jack's cigarette seller friend Golec (Morris Wajcer). The card displays his Polish alias, Stanislaw Kiliniski. Warsaw, 1943. Photo courtesy of the Wajcer family.

2 Jack's cigarette seller friends, including Bull (Irving Milchberg) (left). Warsaw, circa 1944. Photo courtesy of the United States Holocaust Memorial Museum and Irving Milchberg.

3 Mrs. Lodzia. Warsaw, 1943.

4 Mrs. Lodzia's daughters, Irka (left) and Marysia. Warsaw, 1945.

1   Bull (Irving Milchberg), leader of the cigarette sellers in Three Crosses Square.
    Poland, 1945.
2   Jack's smuggling friend Sewek (Sam Weizenbluth) after the war. Place
    unknown, 1950.
3   Brothers Zenek (right) and Paweł (Zalman and Peretz Hochman). Israel,
    circa 1960.
4   Cigarette seller nicknamed "Little Stasiek," in the United States after the war.
    Circa 1950.

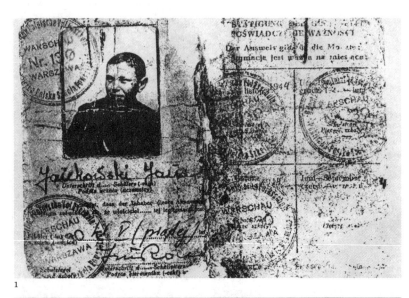

1

2

1 School identity card showing Jack's false name, supplied by the Jewish National Committee. Circa 1944.

2 Identity document Jack used to get out of Poland in 1945.

1 Jack in 1945, likely travelling in Poland or Germany.
2 Jack's musician travelling companion, Lutek. 1945.

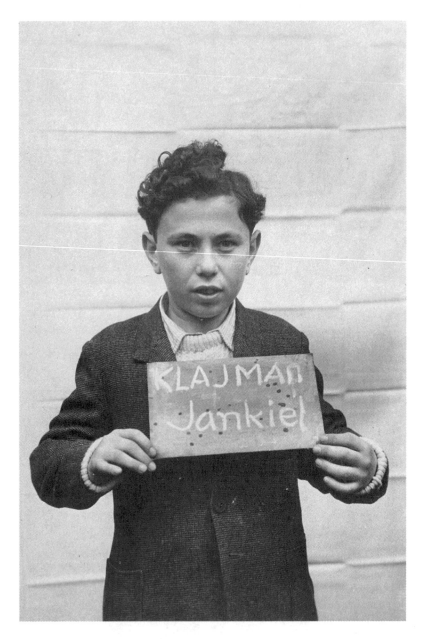

Jack in the Kloster Indersdorf displaced persons camp holding a name card. This photograph was published in newspapers to facilitate reuniting Jack with any surviving family members. He never discovered any family members after the war. Germany, 1945. Photo courtesy of the United States Holocaust Memorial Museum, and of Lilo, Jack and Micha Plaschkes.

1

2

3

1 Isidor Marx, headmaster of the Northampton hostel where Jack lived after leaving Germany. England, 1946.
2 Jack during his time at the Northampton hostel. England, circa 1946.
3 Jack lounging in the grass during his time in England. Circa 1946.

1 Jack continues exploring his love of music while living in the hostel in Northampton, here playing piano. England, circa 1946.

2 Jack continues exploring his love of music while living in the hostel in Northampton, here with accordion. England, circa 1946.

1 Jack (in front, second from the right) at a Chanukah celebration with other boys at the hostel. England, circa 1946.

2 Jack (second from the left) with other boys at the hostel. England, circa 1946.

1

2

1 Jack (on the right) with three other boys from the hostel in England. The dog on the right is the infamous Queenie. Northampton, England, 1946.

2 Jack (far left) playing table tennis during his time living in the hostel. England, circa 1946.

1

2

1 Jack (sitting second from the far right) in school with other boys from his hostel. England, 1946.
2 Jack (second from the front on the left) receiving instruction at the tool and die shop, part of the ORT School in South Kensington. England, circa 1947.

1 Jack playing the drums after settling in Canada. London, 1949.
2 Jack posing with a car, enjoying his new life in Canada. London, circa 1950s.
3 Jack sitting in a car. London, circa 1950s.

1   Jack and Sonia on their wedding day. Israel, 1959.
2   Jack and Sonia on the dancefloor. London, circa 1970s.
3   Jack and Sonia out for dinner. Miami, Florida, 1964.

1 Jack in his fur store, London Klyman Furs Ltd. London, circa 1960s.
2 Jack and his store featured in the *London Free Press*, celebrating fifty years in business. London, 2003.

1 Jack reuniting with Irving during one of Irving's visits to London. From left to right (in front): Jack's wife, Sonia; Jack; Irving's wife, Renee; and Jack's mother-in-law, Eva Dykstein. In back, Irving Milchberg (Bull).

2 Jack and Sonia. Vancouver, 1991.

1 Sonia and Jack. London, circa early 2000s.
2 Jack and Sonia during the celebration of Jack's seventy-fifth birthday. London, April 2006.

1

2

1 Jack with his family. Clockwise from far left: Jack's son Irv; Jack; his wife, Sonia; his daughter-in-law Norah; his granddaughters Nadine, Katheryn and Charlotte; and his daughter-in-law Patricia. Pinery Provincial Park, Ontario, 2006.

2 Celebrating Sonia's seventieth birthday. Back row, left to right: Jack's daughter-in-law Norah; his son Ed; daughter-in-law Patricia; daughter, Brenda; and son Mark. Middle row, left to right: granddaughter Katheryn; wife, Sonia; Jack; mother-in-law, Eva. Front row, left to right: granddaughter Charlotte, granddaughter Nadine and son Irv. London, December 2010.

The Wall of Remembrance ceremony at the Holocaust memorial in Earl Bales Park. Jack and Sonia with their three grandchildren (from left to right): Nadine, Charlotte and Katheryn. Toronto, October 2008.

Jack with Sonia during the interview for the film *Little Heroes from the Warsaw Ghetto* about the cigarette sellers in Warsaw. London, 2013.

Index

158; public transit for, 34
German invasion, xv, xvii, 5–7, 8,
    9–11
German occupation, xvii–xix, 11–12.
    See also Great Deportation
Gęsia Street, 39, 70
Gestapo, 27, 28, 37n1, 58, 112–13, 120.
    See also Nazis; police
ghetto benches, xvi
God, belief in, 77–78, 136–37. *See
    also* faith and religion
Golec (Morris (Moishe) Wajcer),
    102, 121–22, 150, 151
Grafstein Furs, 143–44. *See also* fur
    business
Great Deportation: archival records
    of, xx–xxi; beginnings of, xix,
    43–44, 46–47; informers and, 59;
    intensification of, 48–49; Jack's
    community and, xxvi, 50–51,
    57–58; overview, xxii–xxiii;
    resistance to, xxiii, 47, 49–50, 53,
    57–58, 60, 63–64, 154; statistics,
    xxiii, xxviii, 56, 61–62; Warsaw
    Ghetto Uprising and, xxiv, xxviii
Great Synagogue (Warsaw), xxviii
Grochowska Street, 21, 45, 52, 59,
    104
Grynberg, Isaak (Zbyszek), 60, 88,
    101, 102, 106–10, 113, 114–17, 149
Gulf of Danzig (Gulf of Gdańsk),
    131
Haifa (Israel), 146
Halifax, 141
Hanna (Jack's aunt), 8
Herschel (friend), 14, 15

hiding: Amchu Man and, 103; in
    bunkers, xxiii, xxv, xxvii–xxviii,
    64; Great Deportation and, xxiii,
    49–50, 63; in sewers, 79, 80; in
    Warsaw, xxix; Warsaw Ghetto
    Uprising and, xxiv, xxix, 69, 78;
    history, lessons from, 153–54, 156
Hitler, Adolf, 95, 153
Hochman, Peretz (Paweł), 60, 88,
    101, 102, 125, 150
Hochman, Zalman (Zenek), 60, 88,
    101, 102, 125, 150
Holocaust denial, 158–59
Holocaust Remembrance Day,
    155–56
Home Army (Armia Krajowa),
    xxix, 122–23, 125, 150. *See also*
    Warsaw Uprising
homelessness, 54–55, 59, 88, 89–90,
    92
hope: children as, xxxi; faith and,
    31; family and, 34, 41, 85; Great
    Deportation and, xxi–xxiii; of
    Jewish community, xxi; survival
    and, 9, 28, 34, 53–54, 59, 88, 103,
    154; trauma and, 51
hospitals, 36, 39, 47, 131–32, 138. *See
    also* medical care
housing and shelter: in Canada,
    143; churches as, 90–91, 92;
    committees for, xx, xxxiin14;
    destruction of, 8, 9; Jack's family
    and, 12–13, 60–61; Lodzia family
    and, 95–96, 106, 110, 122, 128,
    151; Slawcia family and, 21; in
    Warsaw, 8–9, 107–8

ease and illness; medical care

public transport, xviii. *See also* streetcars; trains

Radziłowska Street, 92

raids, 49, 50, 57. *See also* Great Deportation

rations, xxi, 11, 18, 142. *See also* food shortages and starvation

Red Army, xxix, xxx. *See also* Soviet army

refugees, xvii, xix, xx, xxxiin12. *See also* migration

relief organizations, xx, xxiv, xxviii–xxix, xxxi, 135

religion. *See* faith and religion

resilience, 28, 87–88, 149–50, 152, 154

resistance: cultural and social, xx–xxi; death with dignity and, 62; to German occupation, xviii; to Great Deportation, xxiii, 47, 49–50, 53, 57–58, 60, 63–64, 154; identity papers and, 102–3; Jack on, 53, 61; posters for, xxi; resources for, 62–63; Warsaw Uprising, xxix, 122–23, 124, 125, 128, 150. *See also* Warsaw Ghetto Uprising

retail. *See* business and trade

revenge, 53, 71, 86, 104

Righteous Among the Nations, xxv

Ringelblum, Emanuel, xx, xxi, xxiii

RMS *Aquitania*, 141. *See also* migration

Romek (cigarette seller), 102, 149–50

Rosh Hashanah, 9

Rothschild, Mr., 137

Rwanda, 154. *See also* genocide

Sammern-Frankenegg, Ferdinand von, xxvi

sanitation, xix, 18

Sarah (Jack's aunt), 7

Saska Kępa (neighbourhood), 88, 103, 119, 123

Schajadala (child), 48, 58

Schmuel (informer), 78–79

segregation, xvi, xviii–xix. *See also* Warsaw ghetto

self-help organizations, xx. *See also* relief organizations

Sendler, Irena (Jolanta), xxiv

Sewek (Sam Weizenbluth), 19–20, 31, 70, 73–74, 80, 151

sewers, xxviii, 78, 79, 80, 81–85

sex, 65, 66–68, 89, 90, 104–5

sex work, 65, 119

shelter. *See* homelessness; housing and shelter

shmaltzers, 37–38, 106, 120, 121. *See also* informers

shoe business, xv, 3, 8, 32. *See also* business and trade

singing. *See* music and singing

Slawcia, Mr. and Mrs., 21, 45, 52, 54–55, 104

Smocza Street, 18

smuggling: by adults, 30, 45; begging vs., 56; blackmailers and, 37–38; by children, xxi–xxii; of children to safety, xxiv–xxv; Jack and, xv–xvi, xix, xxi–xxii, xxvi,

The Azrieli Foundation was established in 1989 to realize and extend the philanthropic vision of David J. Azrieli, C.M., C.Q., M.Arch. The Foundation's mission is to support a wide spectrum of initiatives in education and research. The Azrieli Foundation is an active supporter of programs in the fields of education, the education of architects, scientific and medical research, and the arts. The Azrieli Foundation's many initiatives include: the Holocaust Survivor Memoirs Program, which collects, preserves, publishes and distributes the written memoirs of survivors in Canada; the Azrieli Institute for Educational Empowerment, an innovative program successfully working to keep at-risk youth in school; the Azrieli Fellows Program, which promotes academic excellence and leadership on the graduate level at Israeli universities; the Azrieli Music Project, which celebrates and fosters the creation of high-quality new Jewish orchestral music; and the Azrieli Neurodevelopmental Research Program, which supports advanced research on neurodevelopmental disorders, particularly Fragile X and Autism Spectrum Disorders.